TRAVELLING IN

TRAVELLING IN

by
Monica Furlong

HODDER AND STOUGHTON
LONDON SYDNEY AUCKLAND TORONTO

ACKNOWLEDGMENTS

For permission to include certain copyright material in this book for circulation throughout the British Commonwealth including Canada, the author is indebted to the following individuals and companies:

In the order of INDEX OF SOURCES, 'Travelling In' pp. 123–125

Ch'ing-yuan in THE WAY OF ZEN, Alan Watts, Thames and Hudson and Pantheon Books; BEOWULF, trans. David Wright, Penguin Books; BEYOND THEOLOGY, Alan Watts, Hodder and Stoughton; THE EPIC OF GILGAMESH, trans. N. K. Sandars, Penguin Books; JOURNEYS IN BELIEF, Ed. Bernard Dixon, Allen and Unwin. E. E. Cummings, *love is a place,* copyright 1935 by E. E. Cummings, renewed 1963 by Marion Morehouse Cummings. Reprinted from POEMS 1923–1954, by permission of Harcourt Brace Jovanovich, Inc. and MacGibbon and Kee; THE ARCHE-TYPAL WORLD OF HENRY MOORE, Erich Neumann, trans. R. F. C. Hull, Routledge and Kegan Paul, Princeton University Press; WHO'S AFRAID OF VIRGINIA WOOLF?, Edward Albee, Jonathan Cape, Atheneum Publishers; COLLECTED SHORTER POEMS 1927–57, by W. H. Auden, Faber and Faber; E. E. Cummings, *i carry your heart with me, love is a spring at which, one's not half two, hate blows a bubble of despair into, when faces called flowers float out the ground, what if a much of a which of a wind,* POEMS 1923–1954, Harcourt Brace Jovanovich, MacGibbon and Kee; TAO TE CHING, by Lao Tzu, trans. D. C. Lau, Penguin Books; T. S. Eliot, *East Coker,* in COLLECTED POEMS 1909–1962,

Faber and Faber; Bishop Anthony Bloom, Metropolitan of Sourozh; THE DIVIDED SELF, R. D. Laing, Tavistock Publications; INSEARCH, James Hillman, Hodder and Stoughton; TURNING ON, Rasa Gustaitis, Weidenfeld (Publishers) Ltd. and The Macmillan Company, N.Y.; Virginia Woolf, A WRITER'S DIARY, Angelica Garnett, Quentin Bell and The Hogarth Press, Harcourt Brace & World; REVELATIONS OF DIVINE LOVE, Julian of Norwich, trans. Clifton Wolters, Penguin Books; LEON MORIN PRETRE (The Priest), Beatrix Beck, Éditions Gallimard copyright 1952, and Michael Joseph; Dr. Marie-Louise von Franz, *The Process of Individuation*, in MAN AND HIS SYMBOLS ed. Carl G. Jung, copyright 1964 Aldus Books; Pascal, PENSÉES, trans. J. M. Cohen, Penguin Books; GRAVITY AND GRACE, Simone Weil, Routledge and Kegan Paul; *The Didache* in EARLY CHRISTIAN WRITINGS, trans. Maxwell Staniforth, Penguin Books; THE CAGE, Dan Billany and David Dowie, Longman; PRAYERS OF LIFE, Michel Quoist, Gill and Macmillan, Dublin; ELECTED SILENCE, Thomas Merton, Burns and Oates; ARROW IN THE BLUE, Arthur Koestler, pub. Collins, reprinted by permission of A. D. Peters; THE POSSESSED, F. Dostoevsky, trans. Constance Garnett, Everyman Library, J. M. Dent; THEOLOGICA GERMANICA, trans. S. Winkworth, Stuart and Watkins; GOD IS FOR REAL, MAN, Carl Burke, Collins; E. E. Cummings, *love is more thicker then forget*, POEMS 1923–1954, copyright 1939 by E. E. Cummings, renewed 1967 by Marion Morehouse Cummings, Harcourt Brace Jovanovich, and MacGibbon and Kee.

'Oh, father Utnapishtim, you who have entered the assembly of the gods, I wish to question you concerning the living and the dead, how shall I find the life for which I am searching?'

Epic of Gilgamesh

'Any vital religious discussion in today's world must move, not at the peripheral level of Christian ecclesiology . . . but at the basically existential level of who we are and what human life is all about.'

Alan Watts

TRAVELLING IN

I

I had a dream in which I was standing on a shore like the estuary of a river. A vast iron bridge stretched before me, perhaps a railway bridge. It was rusty, broken, falling apart. As I watched a huge wave came and washed right over the top of it and it was all swept away. I felt triumphant that it was gone.

Another dream. I was gazing into the heart of a great green plant, remarkably like a giant lettuce. I contemplated it. I was drawn into it until I was at one with it. That was all. No action.

These two dreams were what the last few years have been like—the rusting and falling away of parts of one which once seemed full of life, and the discovery or re-discovery of looking.

I have a memory of looking at a rose in the back garden at home—I must have been about two and a half—as I looked at the lettuce in the dream, of scarcely knowing where it ended and I began. And another memory of the huge elm trees there, one fine Sunday morning, somehow invading my consciousness as I lay and looked up at them. What is so surprising is to find in middle age that this kind of consciousness is seeping back to me.

'Before I had studied Zen for thirty years, I saw mountains as mountains, and waters as waters. When I arrived at a more intimate knowledge, I came to the point where I saw that mountains are not mountains, and waters are not waters. But now that I have got its very substance I am at rest. For it's just that I see mountains once again as mountains, and waters once again as waters.'[1]

Perhaps I am at the second stage. What I don't understand is how I lost the first primitive vision, nor why, in the past two or three years, I have begun to recover it. As it is, I wish I could settle down to just looking—at pictures, sculpture, landscape, plants—for the rest of my life. Where nature is concerned it is vegetable life especially where I sense some huge, simple secret which eludes me. I remember going for a walk during a frozen January stay in the country and pausing to look at moss growing on a stone in the wall. And it wasn't just moss but a miniature forest.

I suppose looking is so difficult because the conscious mind gets in the way—it blocks the attempt with its knowledge and its concepts, and its concern with past and future. Children can look because the conscious mind has not wholly taken over. But perhaps we can learn to do it again when we have begun to trust the unconscious processes after all the years of fearing them.

The religious man is the one who believes that life is about making some kind of journey; the non-religious man is the one who believes that there is no journey to take. The literature of the inward journey abounds with warnings about how easy it is to lose the way, how narrow is the entrance and how difficult the path.

What is the journey and where does it take us? What all the

[1] Index of Sources, p. 123.

accounts, whatever their origin, have in common is a sense of the terrors to be encountered *en route*.

There is the terror of darkness and loss, as all that we are familiar with and all that lends us identity is stripped from us. We discover 'dark woods' and 'dark nights', sloughs of despond, and doubting castles, periods where vision and hope vanish together.

There is the terror of infatuation – the encounter with Circe or the Sirens, in which progress is halted as we lose ourselves among our projections, or we play with death and destruction.

There is the terror of foul and unsuspected monsters to be grappled with. Beowulf symbolically fights beneath the waves in a life and death combat. 'The tumbling waves swallowed him up . . . It was not long before the ravening beast, who had lorded it for half a century in the waste of waters, realized that someone from above was exploring the monsters' home. She made a lunge and grabbed the hero with her loathsome claws . . . Swarms of weird beasts assailed him in the depths, pursued him.'[2] His sword, proved in many a battle, turns out to be useless in this case. Only a magic sword, one forged especially for giants, 'too large for an ordinary man to use in combat' saved him. Those watching the lake from above, seeing the water convulsed and bloodstained, fear that the hero may have been overcome.

Then there is a kind of passive terror – the terror of accepting mortality, weakness, old age. Beowulf, after all his years of triumph, has to let a young hero help him kill his last monster. Gilgamesh, the Sumerian hero, dies, having had the flower of life snatched from him after he had given his life to the quest.

Apart from the struggles of maturity which form the journey, one might say too that there is a kind of pre-journey, and that it is this which childhood, adolescence, and young adulthood are about. Ulysses must prove himself on the plains of Troy before the long journey homeward can begin, and then there is the struggle to get free of Calypso who is, perhaps, the mother. He must be a man before he can embark upon the adventures of a man.

Christian in *Pilgrim's Progress* needs his past experience of life to achieve disillusion and the arduous journey which it binds upon him. He sets off running, crying 'Life, life', his fingers stuffed in his ears so that he cannot hear the protests of his wife and children. Dante too realises that he has allowed futility to blot out his early vision of joy and truth. Like most Christian writers he sees repentance and humility as the way to retrace the lost path.

Where are all these travellers going? The Christians talk about union with God, undismayed by the prospect that very few of even the most devout Christians seem to attain, at least in this life, anything which might strike others as remotely resembling this state. The saints often talk of God as a lover, and when they describe union with him they tend to speak (language cracking beneath their feet like rotten boards) in sexual metaphor.

Jung speaks of 'wholeness' and of the discovery of the Self, and this is reminiscent, perhaps, of the journey of Ulysses. Ithaca is the goal, and it is only by a lifetime's struggle that a man may inhabit the island from which he started off. Alan Watts, writing about Eastern thought, describes the dilemma of this journey, one in which a man can get as lost as Donald Crowhurst in the Atlantic.

'The question to be explored is how far out can I get? How lost without being utterly lost? It is thus that when we are children we test the limits of reality, we try to find out how much we can get away with . . . how deeply we can get involved in all sorts of games of skill without losing track. The question for human beings is how *personal* can I become without losing track? How unique? How sensitive and sympathetic? How respectful of human life or, for that matter, of animal life? . . . Is being a person in the direction of losing track? Or may it be that when the connection is lost, it can be regained only by going forward, and becoming personal to the extreme limit?'[3]

Through what country does the road pass? There must be as many roads as there are people, but certain features seem to recur. There is the pre-journey — the establishment of the identity, through courage, through suffering, through success, through love, through battle, sometimes through the experience of being marked, as by conversion or some kind of vocation. There is the need to get free of the mother.

Then there is the embarkation, preceded either by vision or by disillusion and fear. Once the journey has started there seem to be certain landmarks. There are the terrors already referred to, and the suffering which accompanies them. There is an inner struggle between conflicting drives towards perfection on the one hand and wholeness on the other. There is a search to find a true guilt — not the cheap guilt which evangelists once manipulated, now more usually employed by radical reformers. There is the willingness to give up action when it assumes the comforting properties of a drug. There is the movement towards a state of stillness, and a longing for prayer.

There is a new evaluation of masculine/feminine polarity, and perhaps a discovery of some kind of conundrum about femininity. There is gaiety, joy, a sudden perception of a cosmic joke.

Is it a possible journey and does anyone ever reach Jung's goal of individuation, or the saint's goal of union with God, or Gilgamesh's flower that will 'restore his lost youth to a man'. Or will most of us die as Gilgamesh does? 'Gilgamesh sat down and wept, the tears ran down his face, and he took the hand of Urshanabi; "O Urshanabi, was it for this that I toiled with my hands, is it for this that I have wrung out my heart's blood? For myself I have gained nothing; . . . I found a sign and now I have lost it." '[4]

Yet it was the journey itself which was life, not the sign he found and lost again. He had no alternative to undertaking it—it would have been a less glorious death not to do so.

> 'This is the key of the Kingdom:
> In that Kingdom is a city;
> In that city is a town;
> In that town is a street;
> In that street there winds a lane;
> In that lane there is a yard;
> In that yard there is a house;
> In that house there waits a room;
> In that room an empty bed,
> And on that bed a basket—
> A basket of sweet flowers
>   Of flowers, of flowers;
>   A basket of sweet flowers.

Flowers in a basket;
Basket on the bed;
Bed in the room;
Room in the house;
House in the yard;
Yard in the winding lane;
Lane in the street;
Street in the town;
Town in the city;
City in the Kingdom —
This is the key of the Kingdom.
    Of the Kingdom this is the key.'

II

I sometimes find myself trying to catch the moment when the concept of God or the idea of prayer first meant something to me. But what I remember from very early childhood is something that I experienced as meaning; or perhaps something more primitive than meaning — consciousness. I remember sitting in a huge pram outside the door of our house, and *noting the fact*. There must have been many days before, and many days after, when I sat in that pram in that very place, but this time was something special; special in a quite ordinary way. I was neither very happy nor very sad, but I was I, and I knew it, perhaps for the very first time.

There are other moments of that sort of consciousness; seeing the huge elm trees that fringed our garden as living creatures, rather as the cured blind man in the Bible saw men 'as trees walking'; the time when I 'knew' a rose, knew it in my heart and mind where it burned like a small, tranquil fire.

But then consciousness passed into meaning, and meaning was often a kind of fugue made up of both physical surroundings and other people's moods. Thus, in one such recollection, the garden looked a vivid sharp-sweet green, I could smell newly-fallen rain, *and* my mother had lifted me tenderly from a peaceful afternoon nap.

No suggestion yet of anything you could call God, except

the sudden flooded moments of meaning. But it was a tide which retreated as regularly as it advanced. There were the moments of no meaning—moments of fear, pain, rejection, when one lay and gasped for breath and for life. And one had no control either of psychic life or of psychic death.

Pain. The dentist came to our house and gave me ether to extract some aching teeth. I was immensely proud to be having teeth out, and a neighbour presented me with a little celluloid negro doll to comfort me. I came round to an agony of vomiting which went on for hours. I can still see the room where I sat—the wallpaper, the bookcase etched for ever in terror and pain.

Joy. Going to a birthday party for my cousins in Richmond. Having a cup of tea first with my grandmother on an octagonal walnut table, blue willow-pattern cups, tea reddish-black. Me in a silk dress and an ecstasy of anticipation.

Through the winter dusk on the bus, lights shining gloriously on the wet street. My cousins had a Christmas tree, and from it my aunt took a necklace of shimmering, transparent green beads, and gave it to me.

Or, seeing my sister dressed for a school play in which she played Hope. Hope was dressed in apple green with tinsel shoes, and tinsel in her hair. She was so beautiful, and I loved and admired her so much, I felt as if my heart would burst.

Transformation. My aunt showed me a suitcase, empty, uninteresting. She then closed it and suggested that if I opened it again I would find something inside it. With four-year-old contempt I humoured her only to find inside a string of pearls which she had bought for me.

When I was six there was a teacher who kept us all in a state of gibbering terror and guilt, who devised ingenious and humiliating punishments.

We knew that we were wicked and disgusting because she said so. In anger she hit out with astonishing violence—I remember spinning across the room and finishing up on the floor under a desk, knocking my head against the leg of it. She had moments of treacherous sweetness and kindness which led on the weaker members of the flock to betray the others.

"So-and-so has wet him/herself" (no one was ever allowed to leave the room and the tension was extreme). This was the signal for violence, like a pin being pulled out of a hand-grenade.

In her non-violent periods she tied children up, or sat them in the waste-paper basket. Finally they sacked her; presumably there were just too many bruised, sodden, terrified children. It was years later before I could criticise her, feel that I was not at fault, or see the event as other than 'how things are'.

I discovered that I was a writer. I wrote a story with the help of an older girl—I remember asking her how you knew where to put the commas—and was seized, for the first time in my life, by the strange paralytic joy of writing. One minute you are sweating and straining, fighting words and ideas in an agony of apprehension. Then you are swimming in a great, calm sea, in which all is peace and release from tension.

Sometimes, in those interminable years before puberty, I went to church with my sister who was five years older than I, and naturally pious. We went to a very High Anglican church with a white and gold wedding-cake beauty which appealed to me very much. The words were inaudible, mumbled by a priest with some throat affliction which made the whole thing incomprehensible. I was awed and bored, mystified as to any meaning in any of it, and resentful that my mother encouraged church-going as a device to get me out of the house on Sunday mornings.

Yet around this time I did sometimes pray (mostly to be delivered from the terrors of childhood), and I had begun to be moved by odd passages and personalities in the Bible that had come my way from time to time. King Saul, with his periods of depression and his jealousy of David, seemed infinitely closer and more congenial than any of the invulnerable grown-ups I knew. Bits of the Psalms reached me with a kind of promise that life might be more than school, with its fears, its unforeseen and undeserved retributions, its pressures to conform and to succeed. But religion also wormed its way into my fears, and became part of the compulsive, superstitious ritual which was meant to avert catastrophe.

'If I get to the corner before the bus comes, it will be all right today.'

'If I touch the wash-basin once at each side, once in the middle, then each tap, then wash my hands, I shan't get into trouble.'

'If I say the "Our Father" ten times, twenty times, fifty times, before I go to sleep then God won't be angry with me, and then tomorrow . . .'

No one had ever preached that sort of religion to me. I made God in the image of the grown-ups I knew.

There is a shrub with tiny white flowers, the sight of which always brings back to me a memory of marvellous warmth and freshness. It was a sunny day, my mother was hanging washing on the line, the white bush by the back door was in flower, and I came home at lunch-time to tell her that I had passed into the grammar-school. I didn't expect to get into the grammar-school, and was terrified of taking the exam. But a strange, war-time miracle happened. On that same sunny morning I had gone off to school prepared to sit for the exam, and had sat in my place quaking with nerves, waiting for the ordeal to start. Suddenly the headmistress came in and read out a list of names of people who were to be let off the exam as an experiment, my own name among them. It was one of the most astonishing happenings in my life, and somehow typical of the rest of it. The things which work for me never come by trying. H. says that if I get to heaven it will be because that year they have changed the rules.

Stammering. What was it *about*? Anger, certainly. It was a way of uttering one's feelings even while one did not utter them, in what some Scottish research on stammering called a 'controlling but rejecting environment'. Embarrassment. A way of dissociating oneself from an intolerable Celtic fluency. ('She has an extraordinary vocabulary for a child of her years' as my first teachers reported in anguish.) A way of saying "I'm not clever, really. Look how slowly I express myself." A way of saying "I reject words. They persecute me, so I will persecute them."

It is impossible now to relive the adolescent agony of it. A friend once said "You don't *mind*, do you?" and I gazed at her open-mouthed. There was a quote about the effects of leprosy which Graham Greene used at the beginning of *A Burnt Out Case* which came nearer to suggesting the effect than anything else I know. He spoke of the aesthetic disgust which the leper feels. 'Though with time he becomes reconciled to his deformities, it is only at the conscious level. His sub-conscious mind, which continues to bear the mark of injury, brings about certain changes in his whole personality . . .'[1]

The people whom I have loved best have all known some experience akin to this. One of them stammered, two experienced severe maternal deprivation, two were homosexual, one was seriously rejected and bullied by his peers. What made each of them special was not the original wound, but the fact that it seemed to open a door, which in others remains closed, a door which led into a landscape of joy. This does not happen automatically as a result of injury – people can be injured and yet remain unaware – but I know of no one who seems able to talk of this landscape without having known the pain first.

During the two years just before and after I was twenty I had two experiences which led to religious conversion. The first occurred when I was waiting at a bus stop on a wet afternoon. It was opposite the Odeon cinema, outside the station, and I was surrounded by people, shops, cars. A friend was with me. All of a sudden, for no apparent reason, everything looked different. Everything I could see shone, vibrated, throbbed with joy and with meaning. I knew that it had done this all along, and would go on doing it, but that usually I couldn't see it. It

26

was all over in a minute or two. I climbed on to the bus, saying nothing to my friend – it seemed impossible to explain – and sat stunned with astonishment and happiness.

The second experience occurred some months later. I left my office at lunch-time, stopped at a small Greek café in Fleet Street to buy some rolls and fruit, and walked up Chancery Lane. It was an August day, quite warm but cloudy, with the sun glaringly, painfully bright, behind the clouds. I had a strong sense that something was about to happen. I sat on a seat in the garden of Lincoln's Inn waiting for whatever it was to occur. The sun behind the clouds grew brighter and brighter, the clouds assumed a shape which fascinated me, and between one moment and the next, although no word had been uttered, I felt myself spoken to. I was aware of being regarded by love, of being wholly accepted, accused, forgiven, all at once. The joy of it was the greatest I had ever known in my life. I felt I had been born for this moment and had marked time till it occurred.

Love rejected. 'I asked her for the bread and wine of herself and she gave me the stone of refusal.' It's like that.

I became a Christian, went to church, received Communion, argued with the priest. It was like moving blindfold through a place which one very much wanted to see. But it seemed the right way to make the journey – the right way for me.

The priest affected me as much as anyone has done in my life. He was nervous of me, unwilling to say much, locked in his own depressive problems. Yet he was also joyful – he shone with a love and with a care for me which was irresistible. I saw a crucifix in Catalonia which had his face – Christ crucified in simplicity, bewildered by the pain of it, looking down with slight puzzlement into the face of the passerby.

She didn't talk much about speech, but about life, and about Herrigel's *Zen in the Art of Archery* (then almost unknown here). She was beautiful, calm, full of irrepressible laughter.

All other speech therapists began by assuming that one must try not to stammer. She told me to do it – actually to practise it upon people. It was like hearing the Sermon on the Mount – a wonderful admission that one might play stammering, like life, as a game, a gorgeous bit of private absurdity in which one might revel.

J. dying in hospital, and speaking of his illness, rigid with horror, saying "It's been terrible, terrible." Faith had gone, and he could no longer pray. He lived in darkness. Appalled, I found that our roles had been reversed. He had listened to me, answered my youthful questions, borne my scepticism and despair, comforted me. Now I, the child, had in turn become the parent. It's the usual sequence, I suppose.

I went to see her in the nursing-home. They had pumped her out and she was feeling much better. She came down to meet me in the gothic hall and took me to her room. She was beautifully dressed, and her finger-nails were painted, and she made me feel rather a mess. Her room was full of flowers, my own among them, and the nurse brought in tea, and stayed to chat. We were sorry when she went, because the conversation dragged. I was embarrassed that she had attempted suicide, and did not know whether to refer to it or not. She talked about the viscount in the next room.

When I stood up to go she suddenly broke down and said that now her lover had left her she could not go on. She could not go home if his body was not beside her in the bed. She felt totally alone.

I knew what she was asking of me at that moment—to take her in my arms and be her mother. But I was afraid—of making a fool of myself (she had always had an acid tongue), and perhaps of the sexual implications of embracing a woman. And I was in a hurry—I wanted to get away before the rush-hour traffic got too bad—and there were old resentments between us which had never quite healed. So I said something non-committal and went away. A few days later we chatted briefly on the telephone.

A few weeks later she killed herself. I had not stabbed or shot her, nor administered the tablets which poisoned her. But I had let her starve before my eyes.

III

'Love is a place
and through this place of
love move
(with brightness of peace)
all places.

yes is a world
and in this world of
yes live
(skilfully curled)
all worlds.'[1]

'One artist will circle round one and the same centre in his
work ... another type of artist, such as Picasso, will be
gripped in the course of his development by ever new contents and compelled to ever new forms of expression. Yet in
the case of Henry Moore, in this fascination by one archetype
and in the artist's concentration upon it, it is quite possible for
the whole of life to be grasped in its transformations; for every
archetype is an aspect of the whole world and not just a
fragment of it.'[2]

Who's Afraid of Virginia Woolf? One of the great love-poems

31

of our time. 'There is only one man in my life who has made me happy – George, my husband, who is good to me and I revile; who understands me and who I push off; who can make me happy and I do not wish to be happy; who has made the hideous, the hurting, the insulting mistake of loving me and must be punished for it; who tolerates which is intolerable; who is kind which is cruel; who understands which is beyond comprehension.'[3]

A description of that which is better than speaking with the tongues of men and of angels.

'Into a transference a person will bring all his relationships . . . ' This was written by an analyst of the analytical situation, but it is equally true of the transference of the person in love. One of the joys of love is the sense of land reclaimed.

> 'Restored, returned. The lost are borne
> On seas of shipwreck home at last:
> See! In a fire of praising burns
> The dry dumb past, and we
> Our life-day long shall part no more.'[4]

The years that the locust hath eaten are restored. The pain of the old relationship with father and mother is relived, and we are born again, by the charity and wisdom of the lover. A dual role is forced upon the lover, and acted out, sometimes in disguise, sometimes consciously; the infant returns again to the womb, to his mother's arms, to the breast, and is healed. To set off once again upon the journey.

Constable called his wife 'My dearest Life'.

'And this is the wonder that's keeping the stars apart
I carry your heart, I carry it in my heart.'[5]

The gaiety of love, the sheer fun of it. The gaiety between lovers, between husband and wife, between parents and children, between friends. It is the pleasure of something seen, but unspoken, or spoken by both at once, or spoken by one and catching the other's mood. When my friends die I find I miss them most when I think of a joke they would have liked.

I love private languages. Real intimacy has only been achieved between human beings when they get to the point of talking mostly in code.

'Lovers are those who kneel.'[6]

Sex, prayer, art, are about centring oneself.

William Burroughs objects to the dualistic masculine/feminine way of things, and looks forward to a world in which babies can be conceived in test-tubes and from which women can be eliminated. It is the temptation to which all of us succumb in one way or another—trying to remake the world in the image of our own pathology.

Marital conflict (and love) are often about the attempt to correct this tendency. It is our pathology against the other person's. Burroughs would have to 'let the woman in' to perceive the distortion in his thinking, as women have to 'let the man in' if they are not to make nuisances of themselves.

'Till we love, and love discreetly too,
We nothing are, nor know not what we do.'[7]

'Lovers running each to each
Feel such timid dreams catch fire
   Blazing as they touch,
Learn what love alone can teach:
Happy on a tousled bed
Praise Blake's acumen who said:
"One thing only we require
Of each other; we must see
In another's lineaments
   Gratified desire":
That is our humanity;
   Nothing else contents.

Nowhere else could I have known
Than, beloved, in your eyes
   What we have to learn,
That we love ourselves alone:
All our terrors burned away
We can learn at last to say:
"All our knowledge comes to this,
That existence is enough,
That in savage solitude
   Or the play of love
Every living creature is
   Woman, Man, and Child." '[8]

With pain and difficulty we establish our identity as a

person, as man or woman. We are ready to love. Then, in loving, we discover how precarious, how ambiguous, is our personal and sexual identity, as we learn how to play with the boundaries of the self. Eventually we discover the joke, the paradox—the self is only the self when it forgets the boundary. Ecstasy, selfhood, are the moment when we lose the self. 'If a man would follow me, let him deny himself . . .'

There is terror and pain, as well as joy.

> 'The sense of danger must not disappear:
> The way is certainly both short and steep,
> However gradual it looks from here;
> Look if you like, but you will have to leap.'[9]

As we grow older love becomes more diffuse. 'I can love both her and her.' I find myself longing to tell all sorts of people that I love them. And people say it much more to me than in the days when I longed to hear it. When you can say it, and hear it without assuming that love is about possession, it is wonderful how rich all relationships become.

IV

'Without stirring abroad
One can know the whole world;
Without looking out of the window
One can see the way of heaven.
The further one goes
The less one knows.
Therefore the sage knows without having to stir,
Identifies without having to see,
Accomplishes without having to act.'[1]

'In our time the road to holiness passes through the world of action' wrote Dag Hammarskjöld, and it is quoted approvingly by religious writers. But our problem is not that we take refuge from action in spiritual things, but that we take refuge from spiritual things in action. I guess that Hammarskjöld was talking for himself, as a man for whom quietness and withdrawal would have been an easier and pleasanter life than limelight and the agonising responsibilities of the U.N. And judging by *Markings* alone one is inclined to guess that for him the road to wholeness, if not to holiness, might have lain along the path not of action, but of affectivity.

In Church and State alike one sees the results of action severed from its roots of passivity, the quiet brooding joy and agony which is anaesthetised by busyness. Perhaps, like Hammarskjöld, we are afraid of relaxing into life—we dread the pain of self-discovery, and our streak of puritan masochism makes us eschew the joy as well. Keep going—pitiful ghosts of real people that we are—that is the message. The real leaders in the coming years will be those who sabotage this effort—those who know that the road to action lies through holiness and wholeness.

   'The people are difficult to govern
   It is because those in authority are too fond of action
   That the people are difficult to govern.
   The people treat death lightly:
   It is because the people set too much store by life
   That they treat death lightly.'[2]

'In a society where people get more or less what they want sexually, it is much more difficult to motivate them in an industrialised context to make them buy refrigerators and cars . . .' William Burroughs interviewed by Nina Sutton in the *Guardian*.

Yes. But it isn't only sex. It is any intense trans-personal experience which does the trick. What we yearn for (and fear) is the moment of losing sight of our own personality, and this can occur in sex, in love (even where sexual activity is not part of it), in mystical experience, and in various kinds of group experience. I guess that less complex societies were better at achieving fulfilment through the group experience. In our inability to do this, we turn more aggressively and demandingly to sex and to mystical experience.

Burroughs makes all one's optimism feel cheap. 'I think the

whole system is completely wrong and heading for unimaginable disasters. This is unnecessary and different steps could be taken to avoid it, and they're not likely to be taken . . . More and more of our institutions are becoming virus-institutions. Police and so forth only exist in so far as they can demonstrate their authority. They say they're only here to preserve order. but in fact they'd go absolutely mad if all the criminals of the world went on strike for a month . . . ' A Taoist conclusion.

'The drama of Western society is just this: not having anything important to do.'

The search for something to do strikes a note of desperation. The longing for heroism causes men to set up their own monsters, as with the stream of men circumnavigating the world; it is no longer part of a struggle for survival, though it does perhaps indicate curiosity about the way in which the mind responds to stress.

But are all outward journeys really about the adventure within? Is our problem not that there is less to do, but that we have collectively lost our way in mid-journey—a Ulysses who has mislaid Ithaca, a Dante who does not meet Beatrice?

Whereas 'Without stirring abroad
         One can know the whole world.'

Dr. Catherine Storr, writing in the *Guardian*, suggests that it is necessary for lone sailors, astronauts, and others who undertake lonely adventures into the unknown to have something to do with which to occupy themselves. She thinks that loneliness spells danger. 'We all need solid objects round us to learn the shape of our own bodies. We all need the feelings, the opinions, the reactions of other human beings from which to discover what sort of people we are. If these are removed, we are thrown back on ourselves, on our memories, on our imaginations. In a world empty of everything except ourselves, we have to invent substitutes for company, and we are lucky if these take the shape of gods rather than of devils, both of whom occupy our unconscious, our dreaming minds.' Better, she thinks, to have Crusoe's endless obsession with detail rather than 'speculating about the cosmos: in cultivating his garden, but not in challenging God to a game'.

She's right enough about the danger, but if mankind had followed her path there would have been no explorers, either of the world or of the spirit. The conditions of this are precisely emptiness and loneliness, and those whose myth it is to explore cannot evade the monsters. Some are curious about demons, gods, and the flora and fauna which inhabit the *fundus* of the mind, as others are about moon dust. And how much more dignity they have, even the most pathetic of them, than Crusoe, living like a suburban housewife in his exotic surroundings.

'Wandring in this place as in a wildernes,
  No comfort have I
      nor yet assurance,
  Desolate of joy, repleat with sadnesse;
  Wherfore I may say,
      O deus, deus,
  Non est dolor,
      sicut dolor meus.'[3]

'In order to arrive there,
To arrive where you are, to get from where you are not,
You must go by a way wherein there is no ecstasy.
In order to arrive at what you do not know
You must go by a way which is the way of ignorance.
In order to possess what you do not possess
You must go by the way of dispossession.
In order to arrive at what you are not
You must go through the way in which you are not.
And what you do not know is the only thing you know
And what you own is what you do not own
And where you are is where you are not.'[4]

What is the meaning of the old Christian tradition that
the saints in the desert were not attacked by lions, savaged
by wolves, or bitten by snakes? They didn't even have
to pull thorns out of paws; the animals loved them anyway.

Is this because animals (and people) do what we expect of
them? Victims collude with their attackers by anticipating
attack. The paranoid really do get persecuted more often than
other people.

Or is it that the holy have withdrawn their projections?
Wrestling with the Devil whom they have discovered within
they are no longer much concerned with external catastrophe,
whether from human beings, animals, or nature. As the Lao
Tzu says:

'One who possesses virtue in abundance is comparable to a
    new born babe:
Poisonous insects will not sting it;

Ferocious animals will not pounce on it;
Predatory birds will not swoop down on it . . .'⁵

There are two kinds of artist—those like Picasso who are
continually moving and changing—approaching reality from
different angles—and those like Henry Moore who over the
years dig deeper and deeper into the same tiny plot of ground.
Moore's stance is essentially that of the contemplative, who can
find all the nourishment he needs in one or two archetypes. Yet
if a man is not a Moore, nor any kind of creative artist, where is
the fruit of his contemplation? This is what interests me more
and more. When I tried to suggest to an analyst friend that the
contemplative played a passive/feminine role towards God,
she at once replied: "Then where's the baby?"
If there is a baby, then it is the wisdom.

Archbishop Anthony Bloom, in a broadcast, compared the
contemplative to the artist. 'I think a man has the right to the
monastic, contemplative life exactly in the same terms as a man
has the right to be an artist. Not in order to fulfil a function—
not in order to achieve anything—but because inwardly there
is a drive to become what he will become. It may be a comparatively poor product, but it may be Van Gogh, it may be
Gauguin, it may be one of the greatest artists . . . One should
have as few monks as possible—as one has as few artists as
genius allows.'⁶

Looking at Ben Nicholson's painting, one feels that contemplation is only possible in maturity. Only such a strongly
developed 'I' could afford to set itself aside so completely,

42

could attempt such playfulness, or could express itself with such simplicity and gaiety. Two things remain with one after one has looked—an awareness of Nicholson's balance (he has not slipped into false attitudes or self-parodies)—and the light which floods out of the pictures drenching the onlooker.

To be like a bird on a tree, singing in summer, silent in winter, living out one's mood, innocent of drugs and diversions.

'On being asked how to escape from the "heat", a master directed the questioner to the place where it is neither hot nor cold. When asked to explain himself he replied, "In summer we sweat; in winter we shiver." Or, as a poem puts it:
When cold, we gather round the hearth before the blazing fire;
When hot, we sit on the bank of the mountain stream in the bamboo grove.[7]
. . . We do not sweat *because* it is hot; the sweating is the heat.'

Violence is the business of holiness.

Padre Pio believed himself to be in constant conflict with the Devil. In his photographs the look on his face is one of terror.

'All lose, whole find.'[8]

'Our civilization represses not only "the instincts", not only sexuality, but any form of transcendence.'[9]

43

'There comes a moment when this consciousness of the inescapable trap in which we are at once the trapper and the trapped reaches a breaking-point. One might almost say that it "matures" or "ripens", and suddenly there is what the Lankavatura Sutra calls a "turning about in the deepest seat of consciousness". In this moment all sense of constraint drops away, and the cocoon which the silkworm spun around himself opens to let him go forth winged as a moth. The peculiar anxiety which Kierkegaard has rightly seen to lie at the very roots of the ordinary man's soul is no longer there. Contrivances, ideals, ambitions, and self-propitiations are no longer necessary, since it is now possible to live spontaneously without trying to be spontaneous. Indeed, there is no alternative, since it is now seen that there never was any self to bring the self under its control.'[10]

God's a good man, said Dogberry.

I had a letter from a friend serving a long prison sentence. 'The time is now 9.30 and I've just been locked up. You may find this difficult to understand, but I find this period the best part of the day. If I could only somehow discipline myself to spend the *opening-up* period in my cell, I am sure I'd be able to adjust myself to be a more stable person. But, I find as long as my door is open, I cannot voluntarily spend much time in my cell . . . if I am not wandering around I feel I will miss something . . .'
As long as my door is open . . .

'I do my utmost to attain emptiness;

44

I hold firmly to stillness.
The myriad creatures all rise together
And I watch their return.
The teeming creatures
All return to their separate roots.
Returning to one's roots is known as stillness.'[11]

According to Graham Greene, writers and priests are always failures. Certainly there is a growing case for seeing the priest as a kind of poet, like the boy Simon in *Lord of the Flies*, prepared to live and die in such a way that men may discover the true identity of the Beast. But it is a terrifying vocation and you can understand why they want to dodge and become social workers or manipulators in the corridors of power instead. Good priests and good writers should have it in common that they are not public men. They are justified only by their powers of being and of seeing.

> 'Man lasts no longer than the grass,
> No longer than a wild flower,
> one gust of wind and we are gone,
> never to be seen here again.'[12]

'Love does not please until we can somehow cope with it, and we cannot cope with it as long as it is an affect rather than a state of being. . . . The opposites of desire and inwardness, of action and being, are reflected by two opposing traditions of loving which for simplicity's sake can be called Oriental and Western. Holding to the depth and inwardness of love alone is quietistic. Somehow it is inhuman; it negates the living reality of the object of longing by feeding him or her as an image, into love as a state of being to be buried there within. On the other hand, Western charity with its reaching out in contact, its programmes of Christ in action and the Church in service of the community, its movement and mission, soon empties the well, a vain gesture beating the air. If depth without action is inhuman and action without depth folly, then the solution to the split between these two ancient notions of love – as desire or state of being – may depend on the individual analyst or counsellor; to what extent he is able to connect within himself his impulse to extroverted action with his introverted depths. These two opposing movements form the individual cross of love, psychologically seen. For the sake of finding the centre, one or the other direction may have to be sacrificed for a time. I may be able to come to my depths of loving solely through following the impulse to action, living love to the fullest as an affect, forsaking all that I have learned that such love is not the real thing, only a *mania* and a disorder. Or I may have to renounce a powerful involvement in order to take love back into myself, even though I know this withdrawal betrays personal commitment.

'In general, our danger in counselling and in analysis is that of having too short an inward axis to bear the range of our extensive involvements. Indeed, I may love to the uttermost outwardly, but should the vertical connection to the ground of being within myself, to my love of myself, towards myself, by myself, not yet be formed, I will have stirred up a love that cannot please . . . The human encounter depends on an inner connection. To be in touch with you I need to be in touch within.'[13]

'I went to the wood and got it,
I sat me down and looked for it.
The more I searched for it the less I liked it,
And I brought it home because I couldn't find it.'

V

Prayer. The difficulty is how to inhabit oneself.

> 'O would I were where I would be!
> There would I be where I am not:
> For where I am would I not be,
> And where I would be I can not.'

'By the practice of Zazen (sitting meditation) we concentrate ourselves so that we can come to mental concentration even when we're doing something else—reading a book, walking down a street, or doing business and so forth. We can concentrate ourselves through daily practice of Zazen.

'... When hippies begin to sit in Zazen, they often stop taking L.S.D., because they don't have to take any more L.S.D. It's not an escape, but a vision, that they think the drugs give them, so they stop that and sit in Zazen.'[1]

In the West the traditional position for prayer has been kneeling, or standing, though the practice seems to be dying. In the East the position has been the cross-legged lotus one. In America today the young who practise Zen get reduced to tears by the pain of sitting cross-legged for long periods. Is pain somehow necessary in the initial stages of prayer?

What is striking is how in the West we have lost the sense that the body affects the mind. (Though only where prayer is concerned. We admit the connection fast enough in the case of hunger, heat, cold, illness.) And few people talk of the effect of prayer on the body. Yet the changes do occur in a quite ordinary way. The breathing changes, and becomes deep and rhythmic, and one is aware that one *is* one's breathing. In Zen one might perhaps begin with this awareness of breathing, and perhaps reach a point of concentration more quickly.

No wonder the Zen books often seem to equate 'sitting' with prayer. It's rather like what the uninitiated say about writing "If I only had the time I would sit down and write a masterpiece." They don't realise that the sitting down is the hard bit. Giving oneself up to the unknown.

I was stricken when I learned of the Jewish tradition that Moses was a stammerer, a man to whom words are an expression of the inner terror. No one ever fought a more gallant battle with terror.

'And he said, I beseech thee, shew me thy glory.

'And he (the Lord) said, I will make all my goodness pass before thee, and I will proclaim the name of the Lord before thee . . . Thou canst not see my face: for there shall no man see me, and live.

'And the Lord said, Behold there is a place by me, and thou shalt stand upon a rock:

'And it shall come to pass, while my glory passeth by, that I will put thee in a clift of the rock, and will cover thee with my hand while I pass by . . .'[2]

The more I go to Mass the less I understand why it matters to me. It is a bit like Virginia Woolf's comment on her long-standing marriage:

'Life—say four days out of seven—becomes automatic; but on the fifth day a bead of sensation (between husband and wife) forms which is all the fuller and more sensitive because of the automatic customary unconscious days on either side. That is to say the year is marked by moments of great intensity . . . How can a relationship endure for any length of time except under these conditions?'[3]

The only other experience which has ever felt a bit like it is bull-fighting. One is invited to lay conventional pre-occupations aside and trace out the pattern of things. The glory is filtered through repetition, ritual, gaudiness, so that it shall not destroy us. Across this we lay our own filters of boredom, tiredness, irritation and distaste. Occasionally the filters are removed and we are devastated by what we see. Music, prayer, sexual passion—all the great wordless experiences—uncover this terrible pattern. Words are the way of bearing it, and those of us who are most addicted to words are those, in my view, who have felt most threatened by the numinous. When we turn away from words we are making the journey home.

Books about prayer are as unappetising as books of sexology, and for the same reason. It is only from inside the experience that sex and prayer are fitting and fine. From outside they are chilling and incomprehensible. One thinks of the total bafflement of children at the open secret shared by the grown-ups.

What humiliates, looking back at one's attempts at prayer, is the pretentiousness of it all. The elaborate categories which were explained to me when I became a Christian—categories of praise and thanksgiving, of meditation and intercession. One dutifully tried to think oneself into gratitude and penitence and all the rest. I have never quite thrown off the sense of gloom and failure which hung over the whole attempt for me—I felt like a mongol trying to learn Greek. Part of the misery had to do with the talk of relationship with God. I hoped for something not unlike a daily telephone conversation with God, and was hurt that He seemed undisposed to chat.

One's pride and pretentiousness does not much like the alternative, however, which is the scaling down of prayer to something utterly simple, and non-active. Sitting. Trying to inhabit oneself, and to set oneself within the landscape. When one achieves it praise is the natural response.

> 'One who knows does not speak;
> > one who speaks does not know.
> Block the openings;
> Shut the doors.
> Blunt the sharpness;
> Untangle the knots;
> Soften the glare;
> Let your wheels move only along old ruts.
> This is known as mysterious sameness.'[4]

'If thou dost love God, thou dost pray.' Prayer overtakes us.

'Lovers are those who kneel
lovers are those whose lips
smash unimagined sky
deeper than heaven is hell.'[5]

'Worship disinfects our service from egoism.' Henri Bremond.

'One spends 99·9 per cent of one's day not in adoration.' Cistercian interviewed at Caldey.

VI

'The spirit of the valley never dies.
This is called the mysterious female.
The gateway of the mysterious female
Is called the root of heaven and earth.'[1]

'The very fierce animal with only one horn is called Unicorn. In order to catch it, a virgin is put in a field; the animal then comes to her and is caught, because it lies down in her lap.'[2]

A television programme interviewed a man who spent 180 days marooned on an island in South Georgia with nothing to do (his scientific instruments with which he had intended to research had been swept away). He embarked on a contemplative life, and in the course of it invented a woman with whom he held conversations and to whom he wrote poems.

The masochism of the saints. We are accustomed to read of saints starving and beating themselves, or enduring self-inflicted agonies of heat, cold and sleeplessness. The more one looks into this, the less do simple theories of masochism seem to meet the case. Perhaps it is just that we do not know very much about masochism, particularly the extent to which it is 'normal', for instance in a woman's reaction to the man she loves. A priest I know makes the interesting point that since contemplation is essentially feminine, i.e. passivity towards God, then for men it might be necessary to go through a period of parodying and exaggerating female behaviour in order to ease themselves into this unfamiliar role. As it were, dressing up in women's clothes. Once the relationship is secure, then these props can be discarded; the period of extreme asceticism comes to an end.

He was also interesting about the effects of celibacy. He did not believe that anyone could ignore the need for reconciliation of male and female. People who married lived with the fruitful tension of male and female – the 'other' was always there before them in concrete form. Celibates, where they did not fall in love, and where they did not work the problem out on members of their own community, were reduced (if that is the word – it may be twentieth-century blindness) to finding both male and female inside themselves.

Man is essentially a 'peopler' of the world about him. Much Christian teaching about relationships has comfortably ignored this fact, and has imagined that, say, the unhappily married man, or the nun, should be able to live in a vacuum of non-relationship. But this does not happen, except perhaps with the deeply pathological. The unhappily married man either falls in love anew, or peoples his desert with fantasy. The nun transfers her tenderness from men to women, or perhaps to children, or falls in love with a man, or embarks on the more mysterious process (this is what we really don't know about) of finding the man within, thus perhaps finishing up at the place where a really good marriage also ends, in the withdrawal of projection and the sense of personal wholeness.

The surgeon Ian Aird used to say that what he longed to do for his patients in pain and fear was to take them in his arms and hug them.

'I saw the blessed Trinity working. I saw that there were these three attributes: fatherhood, motherhood, and lordship — all in one God . . . God is as really our Mother as he is our Father . . . I came to realise that there were three ways of looking at God's motherhood: the first is based on the fact that our nature is *made*: the second is found in the assumptions of that nature — there begins the motherhood of grace; the third is the motherhood of work which flows out over all by that same grace — the length and breadth and height and depth of it is everlasting. And so is his love . . . The human mother may put her child tenderly to her breast, but our tender Mother Jesus simply leads us into his blessed breast through his open side, and there gives us a glimpse of the Godhead and heavenly joy — the inner certainty of eternal bliss . . . In essence motherhood means love and kindness, wisdom, knowledge, goodness. Though in comparison with our spiritual birth our physical birth is a small, unimportant, straightforward sort of thing, it still remains that it is only through his working that it can be done at all by his creatures. A kind loving mother who understands and knows the needs of her child will look after it tenderly just because it is the nature of a mother to do so . . .'[3]

We have got into the habit of talking as if the primary function of the mother — giving birth, nourishing and cherishing — are her whole value. But quite early in a child's life her function begins to change. She becomes a point of reality, an *interpreter* of what the child experiences so that it makes a livable whole. She is asked to interpret both its inward experiences—its fears, dreams, moods, fantasies—and its outer experiences—its discovery of the world and other people.

As the child grows older, so her interpretations must become more profound. They touch ethical, philosophical, metaphysical, and theological areas of living, of which she may have no knowledge beyond her own experience. But it is the extent to which she has lived what she knows—the extent to which she *is*—which is important to her children, not her intellectual achievement. Her attention and awareness is what is needed.

Perhaps what ails our society is a shortage of such natural interpretation. In a world of experts everyone becomes afraid to know anything, even the things they do know. Knowledge becomes something hard-edged; we have lost the awareness that even the most sober fact is ambivalent and uncertain. The more we know the less we try to make sense of what we know; in fact it is tempting to abandon 'making sense' in order to multiply our random knowing. But motherhood is about 'making sense'.

'With my parents I couldn't be a boy and they never made it clear what else they wanted me to be except that. So I tried to die by being catatonic... When I was catatonic, I tried to be dead and grey and motionless. I thought mother would like that. She could carry me around like a doll. I felt as though I were in a bottle. I could feel that everything was outside and couldn't touch me...

'Everyone should be able to look back in their memory and be sure he had a mother who loved him, all of him; even his

58

piss and shit. He should be sure his mother loved him just for being himself; not for what he could do. Otherwise he feels he has no right to exist. He feels he should never have been born.

'No matter what happens to this person in life, no matter how much he gets hurt, he can always look back to this and feel that he is lovable. He can love himself and he cannot be broken. If he can't fall back on this, he can be broken.

'You can only be broken if you're already in pieces. As long as my baby-self had never been loved, then I was in pieces. By loving me as a baby, you made me whole.'[4]

It is now a truism that this is a period which devalues the feminine. What is meant by this? That we are promiscuous? That we have preferred orgasm to the love which is what it is about? Or that we repress the gentle, passive, warm and intuitive side of ourselves in favour of the tough, active, aggressive and efficient side? What frightens me most is the glorification of activity, especially when it happens in the Church. How can anything grow in us without passivity, the long, dull wait for birth?

I remember the girl in the French novel *The Priest* trying to describe what it meant to her to be a Christian. 'Being poor all the time. Loving people, doing everything you can for them, sacrificing yourself and your own interests, praying to God, taking the sacraments, joining the Church.'[5]

Now I think we should put some of that rather differently. 'Knowing that time is more precious than money. Having the courage to follow the inner myth. Being warm and affectionate to others, faithful to them, free to listen. Loving oneself well

enough to see what one is. Able to *see* – natural things, art.
Able to hear. Able to sit still. Able to *be*.'

Not, of course, in order to achieve some quietistic state –
one might as well take Librium – but in order to bring something to birth and sustain the fierce activity which follows.

If Christianity is to have any life henceforward, then it
seems likely that some rediscovery of the feminine will be
necessary, in both men and women. We live in a world that
has come to despise the feminine, which has only wistful
dreams of beauty allied to goodness, and of generous comfort
and giving.

Literature abounds in spiritual combats and spiritual
journeys, but it is striking that the voyager or combatant is
rarely a woman. Woman is, again and again, the inspirer of the
journey or the task (as she is also often the danger that lurks in
the hero's path), but she is not the explorer. Is this because
women were debarred from literature anyway or is there a
more profound reason?

One other role which was allowed to women apart from
being an inspiration was that of the wise woman or seer. Not so
much the priest – the performer of ritual – though she was
sometimes that too, but the one who 'knew'.

Jungian psychology suggests that if the woman was not, is
not, to lose her way by becoming a maddening crank, then she
must learn how to use her 'animus' or masculine side. The
man's 'anima', or feminine side, is often experienced in erotic
fantasy. The equivalent hazard for the woman is a 'sacred'
conviction. 'When such a conviction is preached with a loud,
insistent, masculine voice or imposed on others by means of

brutal emotional scenes, the underlying masculinity in the woman is easily recognised . . . Even in a woman who is very feminine, the animus can be an equally hard, inexorable power. One may suddenly find oneself up against something in a woman that is obstinate, cold and completely inaccessible . . . One can rarely contradict an animus opinion because it is usually right in a general way; yet it seldom seems to fit the individual situation. It is apt to be an opinion that seems reasonable but beside the point.' Yet the animus, if it develops rightly in a woman, leads her into meaning and true religious experience. Indeed it can go further and connect the woman's mind 'with the spiritual evolution of her age, and thereby make her even more receptive than a man to new creative ideas. It is for this reason that in earlier times women were used by many nations as diviners and seers. The creative boldness of their positive animus at times expresses thoughts and ideas that stimulate men to new enterprises.'[6] But to get to this point a woman must make her own journey, and fight her own battles. Her animus 'must cease to represent opinions that are above criticism'. Her opinions only become worth having when she has ceased to see them as sacred.

It begins to look as if, men and women, we may need to take a particular feminine experience as the analogy of our growth. 'During the Renaissance, many aspects of the story of Jesus were taken up in painting. One particular image seemed to draw the interest of painter after painter, century after century: the Annunciation. There Mary is depicted as a young childish innocent, carefully dressed and set down in a walled interior — nothing more than a schoolgirl at home in her room, often doing handwork or at her studies, who is suddenly confronted with the Angel. In her body redemption will be prepared. She is shocked, astonished. In her face horror and rejection mingle with acceptance.

This motif occurs in men and women today. In that schoolgirl image of our dreams, in those too-young emotions—too naïve, too innocent, too self-centred—something redemptive can grow, which might in the end lead to our own redemption, and to the maturing of the feminine side towards that figure of wisdom and compassion which Mary becomes at the end of the story. But in the beginning it is astonishment and shock, for somewhere we are all virgins, sensitive, shy, psychologically naïve, unexplored in our emotional life, unwilling to be called into involvements, unawakened to the terribleness of truth, resistant to the major challenge, preferring where it is safe, at home, familiar and protected, with books or bits of handiwork, kindly, charitable, obedient, well-meaning. Yet from all this goodness little can come unless the psyche's womb receive the fiery seed of one's own unique essence which fulfils its creative longing and from which inner fertilisation issues the experience of renewal.'[7]

The Shakers caught the joy of what follows.
 ' 'Tis the gift to be simple
 'Tis the gift to be free
 'Tis the gift to come down where we ought to be.
 And when we find ourselves in the place just right
 'Twill be in the valley of love and delight.'

VII

X. talked to me about his alcoholic patients. He regards them as in search of wholeness. Some cannot find it because they cannot achieve human relationships and they need to be helped to do so. Some cannot find it because human relationships are not really what they want anyway. They are after some sort of mystical experience ('Perhaps it is narcissism' says X. wondering if I will contradict). The bottle offers an illusory wholeness—it is a kind of cheap mystical experience, which needs neither God nor other people. Why do people go for illusory wholeness? Often because they are people with a mania for perfection and to achieve real wholeness involves the difficult struggle to let go of perfection.

I do know about illusory wholeness, though not from alcohol, and also the craving for mystical experience. For me, perhaps for many, mystical experience was a way in to loving human beings. If people are frightening it is easier to love God, easier to have a transcendental experience. And you have it and it gives you the courage to make the journey back again and want your wholeness in ordinary ways. I don't want transcendental experiences now. I do desperately want to enter into the ordinary, the present moment.

'Just be ordinary and nothing special. Relieve your bowels, pass water, put on your clothes, and eat your food. When you're tired, go and lie down. Ignorant people may laugh, but the wise will understand . . .'

'In order to arrive there,
. . . You must go by a way wherein there is no ecstasy . . .'
Yes, but 'in order to arrive' you must also go by the way wherein there *is* ecstasy, possession, ego. There must be a self to deny.

How tender Malory is to Launcelot and Guinevere. Launcelot's promises to give up the Queen and give himself over to prayer and penance are repeatedly broken—there is no doubt of the pain he causes—yet Malory never doubts that he is as much on the 'worshipful way' as any of the others. He is even allowed his glimpse of the Grail. He is supremely a man who has renounced perfection for wholeness. He somehow carries the pain of this. What would be appalling in another man somehow becomes infinitely moving in him.

What is devilish about perfection is that it always seems attainable and it never is. It is poor old Tantalus's torment. It drives us to ceaseless anxiety, strain and compulsion. We are like houseproud women. We want the perfect home, the perfect relationship, the perfect holiday, the perfect life.
This kills joy. We need risk, untidiness, chaos in which to refind ourselves. This is what tells us to be forever creating, which means forever denying the perfection which inhibits creation. Wholeness is the only real asceticism, leading us out of the contrivances we know into deserts which we are commanded to make blossom.

Wholeness demands relationship—with man or with God, and often with both together.

Marital problems ought to be discussed against this background of the drive to wholeness. Marriages break either because one or both of a couple cannot endure relationship. Or because wholeness demands some ingredient denied in the marriage.

The social problems are crippling. Perhaps most people tend to marry someone who feeds the immature and dependent side of them. A few years later the couple may be very different from the two people who promised never to part. James Hillman calls this the 'crucifixion of modern marriage'. I think he is too gloomy. Surprisingly often people do find a way through the *impasse*.

Where this does not happen convention tends to pin the blame on the 'other man' or 'other woman', rather than upon the rigidity of one of the partners. (Though to talk of blame at all is usually nonsense—how conditioned we have become to talking about marriage and its problems in a punitive way.)

We seem to need a new gentleness in this area. It is so fraught with fear—the fear of the man at losing 'his woman' to a more virile competitor, the fear of the woman of losing 'her man' to a prettier or younger rival—territorial and survival fears all mixed up with sexual jealousy—that the real issues of love, wholeness, joy get pushed into the background. There is something hideous and merciless about the way our society handles such issues. We are dealing with people's deepest hopes, fears, longings—areas where all their nerve ends are exposed—and violence, the violence of the divorce court, the violence of 'going off and leaving' someone, or what Jung calls 'moral violence' (forcing someone to give up knowing another human being who means a great deal to them) is the medicine offered. It denies the mystery of man and his relationships, his drive to wholeness and to 'become what he will become'. It is this mystery which makes it a sin to judge others.

'Despite the ugliness of ageing one feels more grateful and becomes more graceful, that is, "full of grace".'[1]

I would like that to be true, but is it? We watch the shifting of the planes of our face — what was once taut sags, and what was once full becomes taut — the coarsening of the skin and the change in its colouring — the droop of muscles which tiredness and tension inflict upon us. It is interesting, but bewildering too, because it changes one's external identity. One is no longer the girl that boys whistled at in the street. Prettiness is no more than a ghost, the ghost of a taste (now no more than a ghost) that is left behind when a fine wine has been left too long in the bottle. One will never be *noticeable* any more.

Is it rationalisation to speak also of the gain of growing older? In youth there was shyness and fear towards the opposite sex; neither boy nor girl can quickly make sense of the other's needs. ('Men are so different. It's almost a surprise to find they speak English.') In maturity there is much to be proved, and strange fears and hostilities get unleashed. But in middle age there is a significant change in the relations between men and women. They draw closer than ever before. They have less to prove. They expect less. They are no longer so frightened or arrogant or shy. Closeness, friendship, love — none of it necessarily destructive of deeper commitments —

becomes a wonderfully rich and varied possibility. It is possible to *enjoy* human beings more than ever.

Apart from this sense of love deepening and widening, there is freedom to undertake an inner journey. The woman has had her children and sees them growing away from her, the man has achieved most of what he can achieve in his job. They have arrived not at an end, but at a beginning, the start of the adventure for which it was all a preparation. The bodily changes are a reminder that it is time to be starting.

But what so often makes middle age tragic is the refusal to begin. The man is haunted by disappointment that he did not make a greater splash in 'the world', and tormented by erotic fantasy. The woman cannot cease to sigh for a beauty which she thinks she once possessed (and which, often enough, felt strangely alien to her). They linger around old haunts, melancholy and afraid, forfeiting the respect of the young to whom age can only make sense in a context of knowledge and wisdom, since it is necessarily stripped of other attractions.

Why are they so afraid? Because so few now make the journey? Because there must be a real stripping, a sacrifice of what is no longer needed? Because for men (at least for men who have achieved separation from the mother) there must be a return to the feminine which feels dangerous? Whatever the reason the broad way of destruction is damnably alluring.

VIII

'The good man is the teacher the bad learns from;
And the bad man the material the good works on.
Not to value the teacher
Nor to love the material
Though it seems clever, betrays great bewilderment.'[1]

There is a fine Victorian primness about Lang's Homer.
When Helen is kind to Ulysses in his disguise as a beggar he
says 'This appears very strange to us, for though St. Elizabeth
of Hungary used to wash and clothe beggars, we are surprised
that Helen should do so, who was not a saint'.[2] He means
'How can she be good when she has led an immoral life?', a
curious reversal of Christ's teaching.

'From childhood on men are made responsible for the care
of their honour, their property, their friends, and even the
property and honour of their friends; they are burdened with
duties, language-training and exercises, and given to understand that they can never be happy unless their health, their
honour, their fortune and those of their friends are in good
shape, and that it needs only one thing to go wrong to make
them unhappy. So they are given responsibilities and duties
which harass them from the first moment of each day. You

will say that is an odd way to make them happy: what could one do? You would only have to take away all their cares, and then they would see themselves and think about what they are, where they come from, and where they are going. That is why men cannot be too much occupied and distracted, and that is why, when they have been given so many things to do, if they have some time off they are advised to spend it on diversion and sport, and always to keep themselves fully occupied.'[3] Thus Pascal on the subject of diversion, and he concludes with the words 'How hollow and foul is the heart of man'.

Simone Weil, borrowing heavily from him, discusses man's need to occupy himself with diversion even in the recesses of his mind. Fantasy fills the inner void, which would otherwise be intolerably alarming . . . 'The imagination, filler of the void, is essentially a liar . . . We must continually suspend the work of the imagination filling the void within ourselves . . . The imagination is continually at work filling up all the fissures through which grace might pass.'[4]

I am chilled by the anti-humanity of these two. Simone Weil judges the imagination as harshly as a parent who accuses its child of untruthfulness when, in fact, it is telling a marvellous story. I cannot see how, if we did not fantasise about the future, we could consider our own potential. Nor, if we did not rehearse the past, how we would know our own identity. Similarly we have to play in our minds at love, at sex, at motherhood or fatherhood, at careers, or talents, or achievements, before we can know our own myth and proceed to live it.

In truth, we have little choice, either about fantasy or diversion. If we try to abolish fantasy or diversion we find that this does not abolish them, but simply allows them to build up against our door. Sooner or later they push the door ajar by sheer weight and flood in to overwhelm us. It seems better to submit to the fact that we are animals who need to fantasise and who need diversion, and learn, humbly, to be what we are.

Can it be this that asceticism is about? People fast, go without sleep, abandon possessions and diversions, deny themselves sex, only to discover that they can't do it—that they cheat on the experiment, or find that their thoughts are filled with dinners or girls. We learn from the exercise because it fails, and because the failure outlines our identity more clearly. Joost used to say that Lent was a game; perhaps joke would be nearer the mark. Pascal and Simone Weil are wrong even when they are right, because of the deadly seriousness they bring to religious man. He's a joke and knows it; that's his whole point.

I like the thread of thought that runs through Christian thinking about sanctity, that holiness includes a liberation of the body as well as of the spirit. Beatrix Beck catches the feel of it in a conversation between two devout young women in her novel *The Priest*. ' "There are two things of which I am absolutely certain," I said to Christine. "And they contradict each other. The priest is spiritually the most sublime man I have ever known. And on Sunday, without any possible shadow of a doubt, he deliberately passed close by me and brushed me with his sleeve. You can imagine the effect that has had on me."

"Yes, I'd already noticed," said Christine. "He sometimes does things like that. It's not surprising that he gets bawled out by his bishop."

"Do you think it's just mischievousness on his part, just fun? It must be what they call the wonderful freedom of the children of God. 'Love, and do whatever you wish.' But me, it knocks me sideways."

"He does that sort of thing to goad us on," said Christine. "But of course it's a risk. He's not frightened, though. He's no more frightened of that than he is of anything else." '[5]

An analyst I know says he wishes that the analysts could take over the positions clergy used to hold at universities, which he felt to have been a kind of moral force, an example, a source of wisdom. He felt that the lack of a moral guide-line made for helplessness in a society, driving people either to a total permissiveness, or to a desperate rigidity. I have certainly noticed the rigidity among the young — a left-wing puritanism which can be cruelly intolerant of those who fall short of their political or social ideals, and can be sharply judgmental over homosexuality or drug-taking.

Yet 'the Wisdom' which is what religion is about was only incidentally a moral matter. What theology is about is life and death. Do this if you want to survive spiritually — do that and you will die. It is a map for crossing the Sahara, complete with instructions about clothing, sunburn, sleeping arrangements, eating and drinking, and how to cope with the natives.

'There are two Ways,' says the Didache, 'a Way of Life and a Way of Death, and the difference between these two Ways is great.

72

'The Way of Life is this: Thou shalt love first the Lord thy Creator, and secondly thy neighbour as thyself; and thou shalt do nothing to any man that thou wouldst not wish to be done to thyself.' The writer urges forgiveness (one should fast for one's persecutors), generosity, compassion, calmness, guilelessness, and warns against lust, avarice, murder, adultery, theft, lies, fornication, magic, sorcery, astrology, abortion, infanticide, malice, anger, fanaticism, boasting, and grumbling. 'You are to cherish no feelings of hatred for anybody; some you are to reprove, some to pray for, and some again to love more than your own life.

'The Way of Death is this. To begin with, it is evil, and in every way fraught with damnation. In it are murders, adulteries, lusts, fornications, thefts, idolatries, witchcraft, sorceries, robberies, perjuries, hypocrisies, duplicities, deceits, pride, malice, self-will, avarice, foul language, jealousy, insolence, arrogance, and boastfulness. Here are those who persecute good men, hold truth in abhorrence, and love falsehood; who do not know of the rewards of righteousness, nor adhere to what is good, nor to just judgment; who lie awake planning wickedness rather than well-doing. Gentleness and patience are beyond their conception; they care for nothing good or useful, and are bent only on their own advantage, without pity for the poor or feeling for the distressed. Knowledge of their Creator is not in them; they make away with their infants and deface God's image; they turn away the needy and oppress the afflicted; they aid and abet the rich but arbitrarily condemn the poor; they are utterly and altogether sunk in iniquity.'

As a conclusion the Didache adds 'If you can shoulder the Lord's yoke in its entirety, then you will be perfect' but goes

73

on cheerfully 'If that is too much for you, do as much as you can. As regards diet, keep the rules so far as you are able . . .'[6]

Where we would differ from the early Christians is in supposing that most of these forms of behaviour were more or less under a man's own control. And again we might wonder if there is really any advantage in a man abstaining from outward forms of, say, anger, when inwardly he is raging. (St. John makes the sound psychological point that the man who hates is a murderer.) And this is where the analysts have helped us, and have incidentally undermined the concept of the 'good life' and the 'good example'. Once you have begun to see how compensation works – that you may be generous with alms to compensate for an inner refusal to give yourself, or kind to compensate for sadistic feelings, or conciliatory and timid because the inner anger feels so dangerous – then the old view of goodness becomes too 'simpliste' to hold up. This insight works backwards, too, so that many who seemed secure in their sanctity now look rather rocky. We note the hysteria, the masochism, the schizoid symptoms in what in earlier times appeared miraculous conduct. We note that when Simone Weil starved herself to death she suffered from *anorexia nervosa*. Earlier generations of Christians would have interpreted the cause of her death as heroic self-denial, and have been blind to its pathological aspect.

Two things now seem relevant to this. One is that we may look at the behaviour in the Way of Life much more in terms of 'fruits', as St. Paul called goodness, than as something we try to impose on ourselves by willpower. We will know that we are more or less on the trade route when we want, at least some of the time, to be generous and loving. When we find

74

ourselves hating or taking up astrology, we shall need to see whether we have been misled by a mirage.

And then there is something we have scarcely begun to work out about the way that it is precisely *through* their pathology that men come to real goodness and holiness. Men may fast or abstain from sex because they feel a distaste for the body or for women, yet it may still be in part because they love God. They may ill-treat themselves for masochistic reasons, yet it will be by this regressed side of themselves that (if they can endure the purgation of honesty) they open themselves at length to truth and love. Everything comes in useful—our hysteria, our sadism, our homosexuality. But we have to renounce the idol of perfection if we are to perceive the action of God within us.

'A materialist is a person who loves material—wood and leather, flax and silk, eggs and fruit, stone and glass, fish and bread, olives and wine . . . The cooking of a culture is the real test of its attitude to the material universe, and by this test the Chinese and the French are exemplary materialists. The folk-cooking of America ranks, beyond doubt, with the worst in the world. Its values are purely quantitive, and it is eaten out of a sense of dietetic duty rather than love . . . I would point to such cooking as the main sign that American culture is not only post-Christian but anti-Christian. Proper cooking can be done only in the spirit of a sacrament and a ritual. It is an act of worship and thanksgiving, a celebration of the glory of life, and no one can cook well who does not love and respect the raw materials he handles: the eggs and onions, the herbs and salts, the mushrooms and beans, and, above all, the living animals—fish, fowl and flesh—whose lives we take to live. Ritual is not just a symbolism of formal gestures. Ritual is, basically, anything done with loving awareness and reverence — whether cooking, carpentry, fishing, writing a letter, performing surgery, or making love.'[7]

Envy. The materialist society (using it in the more usual sense than that used above) depends upon it, and it is what rots fellowship and love. 'Loving one's neighbour' means being as glad (or gladder) that he should have something, as if one had it oneself. Most of us can only manage to feel like this about our own children, because we have not begun to perceive that we are as much linked to our neighbour as to our children.

So we feel that others have life—they are young, sexually more desirable, jollier, richer, cleverer, more successful—and we have not, and the pain is unendurable. It *would be* unendurable, if we faced it, so we displace it in envy, and the spite to which it gives rise. The way to avoid envy is to endure the pain inside oneself.

I used to imagine that as one got rid of neurosis so depression would gradually disappear, leaving one in a state of serene cheerfulness. On the contrary, depression when it comes, grows deeper, though the joy which balances it is also more intense. When we have lost our major neuroses, the depression gets less personal—it is no longer principally about ourselves and our problems, nor even of those we love. We seem to go behind and beneath these manifestations of pain and evil until we arrive at a root of suffering, wrestling in terror and darkness with what we do not understand. And then, inevitably, joy follows.

> 'pleasure and pain are merely surfaces
> (one itself showing, itself hiding one)
> life's only and true value neither is
> love makes the little thickness of the coin.'[8]

'I begin to think, after a year in prison, that the only thing that really matters on earth is that a man should escape from his isolation. That he should be able to drop *all* screens and defences. That people should not be afraid of each other. That human beings should cherish the human life in each other, and love all things human. That is the lesson I get out of prison. Love one another. You can't just start doing it, as the bogus Christians think, by repeating the words aloud; the word deputises much too readily for the fact. You have to do precisely what Christ said—throw away all your defences, your goods, your little self-loves which you have deified, and make yourself utterly vulnerable, as Christ was to Judas and Pilate. You have to expose your soul, make the great gesture of trust; you have to cast *all* your bread upon the waters. To be strong, admit your weakness, to be safe, accept all danger. To lose all fear, take off your armour and throw away your sword ... Deny this through fear, and you deny your life ...

'I suppose there are some prisons which can never be broken open—personal prisons, which were first built for protection, but which keep the besieged as fast inside as the besiegers outside—and what if there was *no* enemy, after all? To carry the useless carapace of doubt up to the grave, like a snail its shell.

'But for each man there must be . . . a key to his prison-door. When and if the future turns that key, they will come out at last into the sunshine. Because there is no sunshine unless there is trust and love.

'And that, not intellect and knowledge, is what we turn to in each other. When people do not find my opinion worth their respect, I know it is not because I lack intelligence or knowledge, but because I am shut away from them in a distrust which forces similar distrust on them. And when, as happens more and more here, people bring their problems to me, I know that that is no compliment to my learning. It is better than that. It is a recognition on their part that I am *free* to listen to them, that I am open to them, that I am in some sort a free man . . .

'Do not make tremendous efforts; true escape is not a flight, a running away. It is only when the prison walls drop, drop away from around you, that you truly escape.'[9]

'When more than was lost has been found has been found
and having is giving and giving is living
keeping is darkness and winter and cringing . . .'[10]

IX

The prayers of Michel Quoist. The seminarians love
them and copy them, and in many churches they are widely
imitated. But I worry about the way he uses guilt as a
lever.

'I have eaten,
I have eaten too much,
I have eaten only because others have done so,
Because I was invited,
Because I was in the world and the world would not have
      understood;
And each dish
And each mouthful
And each morsel was hard to get down.
I have eaten too much, Lord . . .

Lord, it's terrible, for I know,
Men know, now.

They know that not only a few destitute are hungry, but
      hundreds at their own doors.
They know that not only several hundred, but thousands, are
      hungry on the borders of their country,

They know that not only thousands, but millions, are hungry
throughout the world.'

Are we really forbidden to enjoy eating, and if we do, does
this encourage us to feed the hungry? (How often I remember
trying to forget or eliminate the friends and acquaintances who,
for one reason or another, made me feel persistently guilty.)
It seems to me to be a kind of systematic masochism. If I may
never feel joyful or enjoy my bacon and eggs while anyone in
the world feels hungry, then I may never feel joyful and
celebrate what I am lucky enough to have. There is also a kind
of arrogance implicit in the attitude 'It all depends on you'.
Mercifully for everyone, it doesn't all depend on me. The
amount that I can take on in terms of loving or relieving the
world's pain is microscopically small. A few friends, a family,
a few people in really extreme forms of trouble, a sympathetic
ear, small subscriptions when I pull myself together sufficiently
to organise them. And I fully expect to discover as time goes
on, that my little bits of love are even less effective than they
feel. The times, strangely, when I *have* felt effective, have been
the times when I have been the one in pain, or the one needing
help. Or when I have had to admit, to people needing more
than I could give, my own helplessness and bankruptcy of
spirit.

But no matter what Quoist says, I am not going to feel
guilty every time I eat my dinner; it feels ungrateful to a good
God.

It interests me that Quoist should be a French Catholic.
Guilt is often so marked in French Catholic writing – is it the

discomfort of a middle-class Christianity over against a deprived working-class?

The trouble is that once you start feeling sorry for (and guilty about) people as a group, you make them to this image, and lose sight of what life looks like to them. (Like a student I know who went to India to feed the hungry and help the underdeveloped, and came back full of a deep longing for the warmth and rootedness of Indian village life. He felt embarrassed and ashamed, as well he might, of what his previous image of himself as the giver had turned the villagers into.) Children in Biafra or in Vietnam, or in Hiroshima or Auschwitz, make the strange demand of us that we give up the luxury of holding them as objects in our imagination. In the rare instances when we can help, we must do what we can. But more than that we must learn how to enter into the heart of suffering, bearing it with, and occasionally for, other people. How do we do this? It is a process, bit by bit, of setting ourselves free from the anaesthetics by which we conceal our own inner suffering from ourselves. In the degree to which we can do it, we can withdraw our projection upon Biafran babies and Vietnamese orphans (admitting that it is the inner baby, the inner orphan whose screams ring so terribly in our ears).

I suppose that only the holy really do this. They withdraw the projections of good and evil from the world about them and discover that the same battle goes on within them. With the greatest, such as Martin Luther King, one can perceive that the struggle moves out of Alabama into the soul, where Christ and the Devil confront one another, where the opposites must be reconciled.

To a large extent, of course, radicalism has taken over from Christianity as the great manipulator of guilt; it's a sort of masturbation of the spirit. I remember at the Marat/Sade (and any number of plays which have followed) the lashing-out at the audience with the charge that the fault for unspeakable acts of brutality was theirs.

What is intolerable for left-wing thought to bear is the thought that pain may prove nothing. To be endurable it must prove that the government is corrupt, that the system is all wrong, or that man is a bestial sinner. But if we care about suffering then we have to deny ourselves the luxury of indignation, and the relief of malice which we can project on to those whom we choose to cast as persecutors.

I don't believe that it helps to manipulate ourselves into guilt, to beat our breasts and proclaim that Auschwitz or the death of Damien was our fault. It makes it easier to avoid facing the things which *are* our fault. One is forced back and back; commanded to save Damien in one's own backyard. To endure real guilt, not cheap guilt.

False guilt, cheap guilt. When I used to answer letters on a newspaper so many of the writers were sick with guilt — about their children, husbands, wives, parents, about existing at all. They had lost themselves somewhere and felt everlastingly at fault, caught in compulsive rituals to appease insatiable gods. There can be no true guilt for people at this stage of development; there *is* no real guilt without freedom and they were not free.

Quoist again. He is so nearly right that one feels a monster to criticise. We do anaesthetise ourselves against the suffering of others—I see that. It is a perpetual temptation to narrow the scope of loving to our own family and friends, to feel that we are justified in pouring out our money upon ourselves. Yes.

Yet if we recognise an imperative to love others then it is no good if we can only bring ourselves to the point of doing it by dramatising the situation. You can dramatise the poor and their sufferings very easily. You can also dramatise the celibate priest, his loneliness, his readiness to give all for Christ. The young priest or the young Catholic Action worker can then be fired into the slums like a rocket going into orbit, full of talk of sacrifice and loving Christ.

The poor suffer from poverty, and the priest suffers from loneliness, but apart from that it is all quite different from the fantasy. It isn't drama—there is no audience to thrill to the pain and glory of it—and the suffering is petty and dull beyond belief. And finally true despair sweeps over the would-be helper as he discovers he is as helpless in the human situation as anyone else. He becomes bitter—he feels he has been conned, which in a sense he has. Priests in this situation often seem to be drinking just a little too much, or to acquire a hard anti-feminine shell, or to become a little strange, a little less than human.

The trouble is that the poor do not fit the popular fantasies of poverty, and the priest does not feel the things a priest is supposed to feel. And it follows that the poor (or anyone suffering) can only be helped by those who have ceased to see them as 'the poor' (or any kind of lumpen mass), and the priest will only be effective when he has almost forgotten he is a priest. The drama must be surrendered. Christianity is not about heroism, not about lashing ourselves into a love we do not feel. It is about making the inward connection, learning to inhabit the square foot on which one stands. There is something so unusual about this in human beings that it acquires a sort of perverse panache. But that is the only drama involved.

X

Life gets funnier; the more liberated people become the more they laugh. Gaiety wells up from within for no obvious reason, and bubbles over into life. Far from quenching it, suffering is intimately associated with it.

Religion is about the funniness of man. It is about man trying to manipulate God and then catching himself at it. I like the way Judaism and Catholicism catch the ferocious glee of it. Protestants, as a friend of mine observes, joke only about other people's sacred things.

Alan Watts suggests that the grace of God may include trickery and fun. He complains that 'it does not seem to have occurred to most Christians that the means of grace might include trickery—that in his care of souls the Lord might use placebos, jokes, shocks, deceptions, and all kinds of indirect and surprising methods of outwitting men's wonderfully defended egocentricity.

'But, alas, the Lord is supposed to be totally devoid of wit or humour. His official utterances, the holy scriptures, are understood as if they were strictly Solemn Pronouncements—not, perhaps, to be taken quite literally, but certainly as bereft of any lightness of touch, innuendo, irony, exaggeration, self-caricature, leg-pulling, drollery, or merriment. Yet what if this show of solemnity is actually a sort of dead-pan expression? If the Lord is said to veil his glory, lest it be too bright for mortal eyes, might he not also veil his mirth—perhaps as something much, much too funny for men to stand?'[1] And he goes on to quote Dante in the *Paradiso*, claiming that the angels' hymn of praise seemed to him like the laughter of the universe. They laugh because we do not see the joy that lies in wait for us, though one day we will. So children wait, in fits of merriment, to spring the delightful surprise which will show a member of the family how deeply he is loved.

XI

She drank it in a wine-glass at 10.20 one bright December morning and after ten minutes felt deeply afraid of what was to come. She felt she might faint, cry, or be sick. A little later she felt hot and asked for windows and doors to be opened.

Time went on and there was a sense of anti-climax. She asked one of her companions — an analyst — the title of the book he was reading. The word 'schizophrenia' occurred in it, and suddenly this triggered off a fit of laughing which felt like the breaking of a boil. Everything was ludicrous. The world was funny, the people in the room were funny, even suffering was funny because no one could see that it was the reverse side of joy. The world was God's joke.

"I see what happens in heaven," she said. "They laugh all the time at God's joke." And she laughed herself for a very long time.

The room had changed. The sun still streamed through the windows — it was a glorious day — but the green William Morris leaves on the wallpaper had become bigger and more vividly green. The sun made a dazzling reflection on the Grant's whisky bottle on the sideboard, and that too, was bigger than usual. The amber coloured curtains looked molten in the sun and her eye was caught by tiny knots and imperfections in the weave which normally are barely visible but which now were big and obvious. She continued to laugh, although she could hear the weakness and hysteria in the sound. Everything was still funny, although she felt alone and apprehensive.

But a great flood of colour welled up within her. Reds and blues, the colours of rich stained glass, filled her mind. There were bubbles floating through water, there were coloured balls, there were whirling circles divided into eight.

"Everything's divided into eight" she said. Pre-occupied as she was with this inner world, she was more aware of those in the same room than she would normally have been. She heard a car engine try to start and fail, and the ringing of the front doorbell.

At this stage there was an almost crushing sense of speed, of moving so rapidly through time or through inner reaches of the mind that there was barely time to describe the landscape. She wanted to hold on to these moments, to savour them more completely, but there was no time.

She was only aware of what the room around her looked like intermittently. At one of these moments she noticed the analyst, sitting at the table, and saw that his clothes and appearance had changed. He was wearing some very coarse material, his face had the pasty look of the very poor. He looked like a Brueghel peasant.

Then began a period of looking at life through the eyes of various painters and periods, beginning with a mock-gothic phase in which everything looked like Strawberry Hill. Then a French classical period of sumptuous landscape. Then an infinitely touching period of luminous English landscape — Gainsborough, Stubbs, Morland — and an awareness of a Keatsian Hampstead. Then the swishing can-can dancers of the 'nineties. "Oh how good," she said, and then a 'twenties scene of rich vulgarity. Finally a vivid recollection of a field beside the school she had attended as a young child. When she was about five she had been so affected by the beauty of the long tawny grass there that she had picked a bunch of it to take home to her mother. There was the field again.

All this was interspersed with pattern. "*Everything's* patterned," she said, and the patterns chased across her mind in endless variety and in magnificent colour.

She began to talk about friends, the ones who would enjoy this and with whom she would like to share it. Suddenly as one was mentioned the whole internal scene darkened. All was darkness and shadow. She was in a concentration camp. Mouths were drawn back over teeth in soundless screams, arms were stretched out in agony and hopeless supplication. The actions were stylised, as in Picasso's *Guernica* painting, but the agony was real. She thought of old people dying in trucks on the way to the camps, of children, with undefended vision, living there.

"I can't bear it," she said.

"Are you suffering?" said one of the others.

"Because *they* are," she said. She was outside the pain, sharing it only because she could see it.

The colour came back in a great tide like a river in which she was immersed and was carried along by. She had gone further into herself.

At one point she passed a great dark tunnel which she did not enter.

"I could cheat on this experience if I wished," she said. Then she began to think about good and evil, and to feel that

89

at any minute she would be able to say what evil was. She kept trying to put out a hand to grasp it as one might try to grasp a swimming fish, but it kept changing its shape. But she thought that the secret had something to do with trying to turn a bit of the pattern into oneself instead of being content to be part of it.

One of her companions put on a record of one of Beethoven's late quartets. First a gay movement which she scarcely heard, then one full of pain and the struggle to understand the nature and purpose of suffering.

When this began to be played she had a strong and horrible sense of vertigo and a feeling of unendurable physical pain. All colour, except a muted pink streaked with a dull green, had gone. She could see her arms spread out on each side of her. Drops of sweat, rain, blood, trickled down her face. There was nothing except pain which retreated only to smash over her again in great waves, pain, and the sense of utter desolation. She had reached the core of suffering — she was *inside* the agony she had witnessed in the concentration camp.

She had reached the peak or the centre of the experience, and arrived on a plateau where time no longer had meaning. She sat up and began to look at the room and the people in it. She was desperately thirsty and asked for a cup of tea. Hundreds of years passed before it arrived, and she was thirsty through them all.

The room was drenched in a piercing white light and she and one of her companions sat and confronted one another like a couple of knights about to do battle. As she watched her opponent his ears lengthened, his eyebrows slanted upwards, and she decided he was the Devil. As she went on watching his face changed continually. One minute he was a clown (he was making a joke), another moment he was a working-man (he was talking of his working-class upbringing), at another a Buddhist monk, at another a psychiatrist, observing but not engaging in the experience. The Devil, she thought, continually changed his face or his argument to suit the situation. She took him by the shoulders and shook him. "Stop changing," she said.

She wrestled with the existence of the Devil, and saw that there was a cosmic tragedy. The Devil had only to submit to love, and there would be no Devil. But he preferred his isolation, his pride. She felt a huge pity for him, not understanding what he missed.

They two were the champions of good and evil, she playing Christ, he playing the Devil. She was not afraid of him. Everything seemed important—the way one even lifted a cup—everything was part of the battle between good and evil.

An hour or two later and all was over. It occurred to her that if one person played the Christ, the other had to play the Devil, and vice versa. She was desperately tired, her head and legs ached, her eyes were swollen with crying. It had been as total as childbirth.

Later that evening she played the Beethoven Cavatina again and for the length of time that it took to play it a change again occurred, though it took a different form. The music fell into huge patterns, visible patterns made by the sound. Suffering and joy were two sides of a coin which was spun and sometimes fell down one way and sometimes the other. In some way hard to grasp in time, the two were the same thing, the warp and weft of living.

"*Everything's* patterned," she had exclaimed, and pattern, and the extraordinary beauty of the paintings were her abiding memories of the experience. A day or two later, she went to a number of art galleries and looked at paintings by some of the same masters and of the same periods. She was bitterly disappointed. The perfection was not there. The works (some of which she had loved in the past) seemed dead, amateurish, pathetic. Life had gone out of them.

Her final verdict on it all was that she had had a profoundly moral experience, perhaps the deepest she had ever known. It involved a kind of repentance, since it demanded that she admit how much she had starved her 'being' side of the stillness it needed in order to feed the desire for action. The way forward was to go back to roots and begin again.

XII

Tom Merton lived as a hermit at the end of his life. He said one of the advantages was that he could sing while he cooked his breakfast. He sang a song called 'Silver Dagger'. He did not look ascetic. He was broad, weather-beaten, a bit on the plump side, with a face like an Irish navvy. After twenty years of stability in Kentucky, he went to Bangkok to a conference, and died from heart failure after touching a faulty electric fan. He was on his way to Japan, to the Zen communities whose unintense beliefs had taught him so much. "He would have been amused at such a Zen-like death," said one of his friends.

'What happened to Thomas Merton?' is what I wonder. He joined the Cistercian order as a young man beset by considerable problems who wore an aggressive Catholicism like a glaring birthmark. For several years before his death he wrote with a freedom, a peace, and a total *awareness* of the contemporary situation which I cannot easily explain.

I went back to reading *Elected Silence* recently. I remembered being first awed, and finally exasperated by it twenty years ago. He agonises tediously over his sins (which are the usual ones), he is full of the anti-Protestant gibes which were so popular then and seem so repulsive now. Of his Protestant baptism he remarks 'I don't think there was much power in the waters of the baptism I got in Prades, to untwist the warping of my essential freedom, or loose me from the devils that hung like vampires on my soul.' Tiresome from several points of view. Of the Protestant school at Montauban to which he was nearly sent, he remembers it as a nice building, but thanks God he was never sent there. Of a Catholic school at St. Antonin to which he was also never sent, he remembers the boys as 'exceptionally nice fellows, very pleasant and good'. All that is Catholic is good. All else is evil, including cinemas (he really does hate the movies), the life of a big city, his grandparents (who gave him a home when he needed it and a good deal of love, but who were not Catholic or even religious), and, in the pre-Catholic days, himself.

By contrast, when he enters the Abbey of Gethsemani, all is white, pure and lovely. 'The place smelled frighteningly clean; polished and swept and repainted and repainted over and over, year after year.' (Throughout the book, all Catholic establishments have a way of being 'frighteningly clean'.) And the Cistercians are no ordinary Christians, but something much more special. As he says in a prayer addressed to the Queen of Heaven 'It is very true that the Cistercian Order is your special territory and that those monks in white cowls are your special servants, *servitores Sanctae Mariae . . .* And of all things, it is the Rules of the Religious Orders dedicated to you that are loudest and truest in proclaiming your honour, and your greatness obliquely by the sacrifices that love of you drives men to make. So it is that the Usages of the Cistercians are a Canticle for your glory, Queen of Angels, and those who live those Usages proclaim your tremendous prerogatives louder than the most exalted sermons.'

Upheld by this sense of 'specialness' Thomas Merton enters Gethsemani. The dirty, noisy, wicked, non-Catholic world is left to stew in its own filthy juice.

He sees no fault anywhere. The monks, the novices, his superiors, the buildings, the grounds, the liturgy are all that they should be. He converts his brother, later killed in the war. He relishes every painful detail of life in the monastery. And the book ends, though not before, almost casually, he has voiced his terrible suspicion that the devil may have squeezed in behind him through the monastery door.

'By this time I should have been delivered of any problems about my true identity . . . But then there was this shadow, this double, this writer who had followed me into the cloister. He is still on my track. I cannot lose him. He still wears the name of Thomas Merton. Is it the name of an enemy? He is supposed to be dead. But he stands and meets me in the doorway of all my prayers, and follows me into church. He kneels with me behind the pillar, this Judas, and talks to me all the time in my ear.

'He is a business man. He is full of ideas. He generates books in the silence that ought to be sweet with the infinitely productive darkness of contemplation.

'And the worst of it is, he has my superiors on his side.

'Nobody seems to understand that one of us has got to die. sometimes I am mortally afraid . . .'[1]

This was the old Thomas Merton, best-selling Catholic author, beloved of the Waughs and Greenes. (In the early 'fifties, I remember how Duckett's window was always full of Merton's books. I went in there the other day to see if they could locate any American editions of his essays, and there

95

were only two of his vast output of books, hidden away in a corner.) Waugh's Foreword to *Elected Silence* joins Merton in washing its hands of the modern world. 'The modern world is rapidly being made uninhabitable . . . We are back in the age of Gregory, Augustine and Boniface, and in compensation the Devil is being disarmed of many of his former enchantments. Power is all he can offer now; the temptations of wealth and elegance no longer assail us. As in the Dark Ages the cloister offers the sanest and most civilised way of life.' He calls the book a 'classic record of spiritual experience'.

Graham Greene gave his two cents' worth. 'It is a book one reads with a pencil so as to make it one's own.' John Betjeman liked it. Malcolm Muggeridge, writing in the *Daily Telegraph*, said 'He has notably and usefully succeeded in presenting in contemporary idiom his reaction against a prevailing spirit of materialism and futility'.

What happened to Thomas Merton after that? Outwardly everything remained much the same. Merton lived out the grim rigour of being a Trappist. He wrote books about it which were progressively less interesting, which bore the marks of having been written either from habit or out of obedience rather than a passion to communicate. *Elected Silence* (published in a slightly different form in America under the title of *Seven Storey Mountain*) was a best-seller.

It is the inner journey that is interesting. This is charted in an essay called *The Cell* which he wrote years later and in which the peculiar problems of solitude and contemplation are dramatised by stories of the Desert Fathers. He begins movingly with the story of the *akedia* of a young monk.

'A brother asked one of the Elders saying: What shall I do,

Father, for I work none of the works of a monk but here I am in torpor, eating and drinking and sleeping and in bad thoughts and in plenty of trouble, going from one struggle to another and from thoughts to thoughts. Then the old man said: Just you stay in your cell and cope with all this as best you can without being disturbed by it. I would like to think that the little you are able to do is nevertheless not unlike the great things that Abba Anthony did on the mountain, and I believe that if you sit in your cell for the Name of God and if you continue to seek the knowledge of him, you too will find yourself in the place of Abba Anthony.'

Merton's comment on this is that to 'sit in the cell' or to 'learn from the cell' means learning 'that one is not a monk'. It meant that the disciple was opening up to the fruitful lessons of solitude. 'But in the disciple's own mind this experience was so defeating and confusing that he could only interpret it in one way; as a sign that he was not called to this kind of life. In fact, in any vocation at all, we must distinguish the grace of the call itself from the preliminary image of ourselves which we spontaneously and almost unconsciously assumed to represent the truth of our calling. Sooner or later this image must be destroyed and give place to the concrete reality of the vocation *as lived* in the actual mysterious plan of God, which necessarily contains many mysterious elements we could never have foreseen.'

The disciple (Merton) plunges ever more deeply into depression. There is the agony of a fixed situation in which no kind of *divertissement* is possible.

'My thoughts torment me saying you cannot fast or work, at least go and visit the sick for this also is love.' The Elder replies 'Go on, eat, drink, sleep, only do not leave your cell.'

The disciple's misery and boredom increases. According to Merton he 'represents to himself a more fruitful and familiar way of life, in which he appears to himself to "be someone" and to have a fully recognisable and acceptable identity, a "place in the Church", but the Elder tells him that his place in the Church will never be found by following these ideas and images of a plausible identity. Rather it is to be found by travelling in a way that is new and disconcerting because it has never been imagined by us before, or at least we have never conceived it as useful or even credible for a true Christian. A way in which we seem to lose our identity and become nothing. Patiently putting up with the incomprehensible unfulfilment of the lonely, confined, silent, obscure life of the cell, we gradually find our place, the spot where we belong as monks ... This implies a kind of mysterious awakening to the fact that *where we actually are is where we belong* ... Suddenly we see "This is IT".'[2]

This awareness, which Merton elsewhere calls 'nowness', flowers from a situation impossible to live in, a miraculous bloom out of dry soil. The soul acknowledges despair, blindness, unawareness of God, limitations which nail it unwillingly upon the present moment. It submits, not in bitterness but in the only tiny movement of love and trust left within it, and the desert blossoms like the rose.

The Christian life can all be done on the spot. On this square foot of ground on which we stand we experience crucifixion and resurrection (if we are not so taken up with manipulating life that nothing can happen to us), and this is action, the action of love. It does not matter whether we do it in the solitude of a cell or in the New York subway. Only the moment matters. That is where God is.

It was not surprising that when his thoughts had moved in this direction (by about 1953 there is evidence of it in his writings) Merton should move on to a feeling for Zen which also thinks timelessness is to be found in the present moment.

He acquired very different friends from Waugh and Greene. The Catholic Worker group began to regard him as a kind of guru. Joan Baez and others of the Civil Rights Movement began to turn to him. Martin Luther King arranged to come and stay at Gethsemani to talk and rest. Merton became totally ecumenical in outlook, but he was now as interested in world politics as he had once been in the minutiae of Cistercian history. He left his enclosure at times. A friend remembers taking him to the nearby Shaker village in Kentucky (he had a deep interest in the Shakers) where he was recognised at once by one of the people there.

On the way back to Gethsemani in the evening they heard over the car radio that Martin Luther King had been shot and Merton insisted that they should stop on the way home and visit a negro friend of his, who kept a small restaurant in Bardstown, and spend the evening with him.

Merton could not really be said to be a Vatican II man. He had achieved liberation by his own route before then, and his mind had already moved away from specifically Catholic problems to wrestle with the much graver issues of good and evil on which mankind is hung up.

The friend who visited the Shakers with him points out that the title of his last book *Conjectures of a Guilty Bystander* (1968) maps his psychological journey. When he entered Gethsemani wickedness got left at the door. The mature Tom Merton had taken the badness back into himself. He did not have to be perfect any more. He had learned from contemplation that we have to withdraw the projections of evil that we place upon individuals, and groups, and nations, and endure the discovery that the Devil is within us.

In his later years he did not like *Elected Silence* very much and was depressed to learn that it was still selling. He went on working at being a monk. His last book was called *The Climate of Monastic Prayer*. He was attending a conference on monastic life at the time when he died. But he no longer thought or wrote as if the Cistercians were a superior caste. He wondered sometimes, as people do nowadays, if this really was the right way to serve the world or God. He got exasperated by the harm that religious obedience can do to personalities which already lack sufficient initiative and autonomy. He loved a very large number of people, and was spontaneous in expressing affection. He was a very good man.

XIII

Blythburgh in winter. The inside of the church is like an enclosed courtyard with high white walls. You can smell the damp and the loneliness. The great wooden angels stare uncaringly down. There is a large metal stove pulled out into the aisle to heat the church on Sundays. On weekdays it is too cold to sit still.

In summer it is full of visitors. C. climbed up a little staircase and looked through the pointed aperture at the top. Her long hair hung down on each side of her face. "Look," said A. "like a princess." You can see the tower miles away as you walk across the marshes among the flowering broom and the brown reed-beds. The reeds make a tapping noise when the wind blows and they break up into a mass of dots like a *pointilliste* painting. In Suffolk the sky fills three-quarters of the landscape; the fresh colour of it is constantly changing, and the perpetual movement of the clouds is drama. At home I scarcely see the sky.

D. told me of a friend who visited a hermit on Aegina. The man had come with urgent problems to discuss but when he got there he found the hermit's little hut crammed with clocks, clocks of every possible shape and size, which chimed and ticked until conversation seemed impossible. Worse than that, instead of paying attention, the hermit kept leaping up to adjust them, and gave only half his attention to his visitor. Eventually though, the meeting was a success, and the visitor found the help he needed. When he left the hermit came to see him off and said "You *were* shocked by my clocks, weren't you?"

Wales. Lambs, very white in a pale green field full of purple thistles, which grow at regular intervals like Pre-Raphaelite lilies. The sheep in the pasture against the fence eat all the time. If you go out of the cottage you can hear hundreds of mouths pulling and munching grass. The red bog. In July it is full of cotton grass with silky white tufts. Where the bog is treacherous the moss is a livid yellow colour. There are hundreds of lapwings over the pastures and their white breasts and black throats give a beautiful striped effect when they fly. Their wings flap slowly and they call out. Lots of owls. They sit on the telegraph poles, and the babies run along the road in front of us. We passed a falcon in the Cambrians. It turned and stared furiously, not at all afraid.

The men on the farms have pink and white skins like girls. They work in the fields in old lounge suits—somehow a sign of real, though dignified poverty.

She was the wife of a Norwegian farmer, and she listened bewildered to all the Swedish talk of men caring for the children part of the day while women pursued their own careers.

"When my child is sick," she said "he wants this . . . and this" and she pointed to her arm and her breast.

Stockholm on a Saturday afternoon. Just as the taxi was starting, a drunk, very respectably dressed, reeled across the pavement and threw himself across the bonnet. The driver had to get out and push him off. Two more drunks came up to me as I went to buy a ticket at the station, offering me a drink from their bottle.

A. dancing to the gramophone when he was about three, and suddenly stopping. "I don't like the thought of dying," he said.

She talked about Russia in the old days.
"People couldn't go to church very often. The distances are so vast. In winter there was the snow. In spring the floods, and the mud which they leave behind. In summer the heat and the clouds of dust. Churches were often built on hills where the faithful could see them from miles away. They followed the service in their books, knew where the priest had got to by the ringing of the bells."
Her upbringing had been ecumenical. The family were Orthodox, but there had been French and German governesses who were Catholic and Protestant, servants from parts of Russia which were Old Believer. As a child she had thought of God as "He who understands".
"I spent a lot of time in Bolshevik prisons. Sharing a cell was the worst. I used to long for solitary confinement."

H., who was brought up in a devout Jewish household, said

that for a long time he nourished the childish hope that he
might turn out to be the Messiah.

A medieval Catalonian crucifix. Desperately moving because
the Christ had such enormous feet.

XIV

'About suffering they were never wrong,
The Old Masters: how well they understood
Its human position; how it takes place
While someone else is eating or opening a window
    or just walking dully along;
How, when the aged are reverently, passionately waiting
For the miraculous birth, there always must be
Children who did not specially want it to happen, skating
On a pond at the edge of the wood:
They never forgot
That even the dreadful martyrdom must run its course
Anyhow in a corner, some untidy spot
Where the dogs go on with their doggy life and the
    torturer's horse
Scratches its innocent behind on a tree.'[1]

The loneliness of suffering. While Christ sweats in Gethsemane others are making love, or doing their accounts, or cooking the supper. Necessarily.

The suffering of children. I shall never go back and read the passage in *The Brothers Karamazov* about the child who was hunted to death by the master and his hounds, but there is no need. As Dostoevsky himself discovered, one can read daily in the newspapers of the agony of children. A little girl is slowly crushed in a lift. A party of French school-children picnicking on a sand-bank in the Loire, are washed into the river and drowned, to be found clutching one another in helpless terror. A six-year-old girl sees a man stab her mother to death while she is being taken to school. A thirteen-year-old girl is kept prisoner for months by a kidnapper, and is finally discovered starved or asphyxiated after the man's death. Hundreds of children are suffocated and crushed beneath the slag-heaps of Aberfan. Christ is crucified daily before us.

'Thalidomide child has I.Q. of 123. Richard, aged seven, born without arms, was an extremely wearing and difficult child to care for, the judge was told by a consultant physician. His mother had said she frequently felt unreal, in a dream, that there was no future . . . The judge's decision will act as a guide in settling some sixty outstanding cases . . .'

Guardian 16.7.69.

'Ian Cox is ten years old. He was playing in some rubble in Caernarvon four days after the Investiture. A time-bomb hidden in the rubble exploded. And this innocent, cheerful boy is now lying in hospital in a very serious condition. His right foot has had to be amputated . . .'

Daily Mail July, 1969.

'When my son of fifteen caught ideas about pupil power over Easter, we stopped his plans to spread them very simply. By putting him back into short trousers. Dressed at school like a first-former, in cap, blazer, grey shorts and stockings with coloured turnover tops, his political speeches cut no ice. At home, bare knees remind him effectively he is still a youngster and he now gives us very little trouble.'

Letter in *Daily Mail*.

In Jerusalem, at the fortress called the Antonia, a little nun led me out on to the Roman pavement where Christ stood before Pilate. On the stones you can see marks carved for a game rather like crown and anchor. Part of the game included bringing in a slave, making him 'king', and knocking him about.

'They clothed him with purple, and platted a crown of thorns, and put it about his head. And began to salute him, Hail, King of the Jews! And they smote him on the head with a reed, and did spit upon him, and bowing their knees worshipped him.

'And when they had mocked him, they took off the purple from him, and put his own clothes on him, and led him out to crucify him.'

Arthur Koestler, wrestling with the transcendent quality of suffering in Europe in the past forty years coins the word Ahor—Archaic Horror—to describe it. He first discovered it as a five-year-old child when he was taken by the parents he loved and trusted on an apparently routine visit to the doctor. Innocently he sat down in the doctor's chair, and suddenly found himself strapped to it. His parents were ushered out, and the child was derelict and alone.

'There followed several indelible moments of steel instruments being thrust into the back of my mouth, of choking and vomiting blood into the tray beneath my chin; then two more attacks with the steel instruments and more choking with blood and vomit. This is how tonsillectomies were performed, without anaesthetic, A.D. 1910 in Budapest . . . Those moments of utter loneliness, abandoned by my parents, in the grip of a hostile and malign power, filled me with a kind of cosmic terror. It was as if I had fallen through a manhole into a dark underground world of archaic brutality. Thenceforth I never lost my awareness of the existence of that second universe into which one might be transported, without warning, from one moment to the other. The world had become ambiguous, invested with a double meaning; events moved on two different planes at the same time—a visible and an invisible one— like a ship which carries passengers on its sunny decks, while its keel ploughs through the dark phantom world beneath.' The experience was to repeat itself for Koestler. 'When years later I fell into the hands of the regime which I dreaded and detested most, and was led in handcuffs through a hostile crowd, I had the feeling that this was but a repetition of a situation I had already lived through—that of being tied, gagged and delivered to a malign power.'[2]

Like Koestler, I stumbled by accident, at an early age, into the world of Ahor. It is all about us from hour to hour—the physical agony as the human body with its exquisite network of nerves is burned, crushed, torn, starved, or rots while the consciousness remains intact. The mental agony as men suffer rejection, spite, ridicule, cruelty, hate, and the frail sense of a lovable identity is ripped from them, the only rag left to cover their psychic nakedness.

Calvary never stops. Christ is crucified in his little ones

unceasingly. We see the Lord abandoned wherever we look.

Later I slipped equally accidentally into the opposite of Ahor. The experience seemed as total, as authentic; this time everything moved in a pattern of joy and light. God was present as utterly, unequivocally, fulfillingly, as he had been absent from the earlier experience.

God absent and God present. The crucifixion and the resurrection.

Increasingly as one learns to part the fibres of grown-up suffering one perceives the lost child, and hears its piercing cry. We can hear and be fully merciful to it only when we come to see that we are moved because it echoes the lost child within us.

'Sing, O barren, thou that didst not bear; break forth into singing, and cry aloud, thou that didst not travail with child: for more are the children of the desolate than the children of the married wife, saith the Lord.

'Enlarge the place of thy tent, and let them stretch forth the curtains of thine habitations: spare not, lengthen thy cords, and strengthen thy stakes; for thou shalt break forth on the right hand and on the left; and thy seed shall inherit the Gentiles, and make the desolate cities to be inhabited.

'Fear not; for thou shalt not be ashamed: neither be thou confounded; for thou shalt not be put to shame: for thou shalt forget the shame of thy youth, and shalt not remember the reproach of widowhood any more.

'For thy Maker is thine husband; the Lord of hosts is his name; and thy Redeemer the Holy One of Israel . . .

'For the Lord hath called thee as a woman forsaken and

grieved in spirit, and a wife of youth, when thou wast refused, saith thy God.

'For a small moment have I forsaken thee; but with great mercies will I gather thee . . .

'For the mountains shall depart, and the hills be removed; but my kindness shall not depart from thee, neither shall the covenant of my peace be removed, said the Lord that hath mercy on thee.

'O thou afflicted, tossed with tempest, and not comforted, behold, I will lay thy stones with fair colours, and lay thy foundations with sapphires . . . And all thy children shall be taught of the Lord; and great shall be the peace of thy children.'[3]

The theme of the barren woman is one which recurs hauntingly throughout the Bible, as is also the theme of reparation for what seems irreparable loss. 'And I will restore to you the years that the locust hath eaten . . .'[4]

The question must be, for those who are afflicted, tossed with tempest and not comforted, whether any of this is more than Jewish wishful thinking. The barren woman is not interested in the delights that are to come; she needs a baby in her arms *now*, and the fulfilment of being a mother.

Yet she is not merely to be fulfilled—she is to be *more* fulfilled than the ordinary mother. 'More are the children of the desolate than the children of the married wife.'

What are we to say of our own bitterest disappointments and other peoples? We can only speak with caution of other people's pain, since we cannot glibly assume that the barrenness will be fruitful. They may insist on bitterness, as we may ourselves.

Yet E., who spent his late adolescent years in a concentration camp, said to me once that he had come to believe that the present could change the past. If healing took place in the unconscious, and the unconscious is, as he believed, outside time, then the past could be changed. The years of the locust really could be restored.

I find it easier to think in terms of perspective. As I look back over past years I cannot help noticing how relieved I am that many old longings never found fulfilment. So that it does not seem impossible that one day one will arrive at a perspective from which all one's hurts make sense. Would I say that if I had watched a child die from cancer, or if I had not had a child at all? Not yet, but I have faith that in a different, later perspective, my own agony and even the agony of others would exact from me a willing assent. This, I think, was what happened to Job.

But this is not quite all. It is somehow the very fact of her barrenness which finally makes the woman so gloriously fruitful. We do not find life and joy in spite of our agony and frustration, but somehow in it and because of it. The tree of our crucifixion bursts into flower.

> 'What if a dawn of a doom of a dream
> bites this universe in two,
> peels forever out of this grave
> and sprinkles nowhere with me and you?
> Blow soon to never and never to twice
> (blow life to isn't, blow death to was)
> —all nothing's only our hugest home;
> the most who die, the more we live.'[5]

III

The H-bomb outside, the darkness within—there's nothing to choose between them for terror. But the reverse side of terror and pain is joy—it is the scandal of Christianity.

' "Everything's good."

' "Everything?"

' "Everything. Man is unhappy because he doesn't know he's happy. It's only that. That's all, that's all! If any one finds out, he'll become happy at once, that minute . . . It's all good. I discovered all of a sudden."

' "And if anyone dies of hunger, and if anyone insults and outrages the little girl, is that good?"

' "Yes! And if anyone blows out his brains for the baby, that's good. And if he doesn't, that's good, too. It's all good, all. It's good for all those who know it's all good. If they knew that it was good for them, it would be good for them, but as long as they don't know it's good for them, it will be bad for them. That's the whole idea, the whole of it." '[6]

In the village of Wenhaston they have a painting called a Doom which used to hang over the chancel arch of the church, but which now hangs on a side wall. In the centre of the painting was Christ on the cross. Below it on each side were grim reminders of hell-fire.

It is similar to Continental paintings of the same period. Monastic artists across Europe had a style as uniform as that of Hollywood in the 'thirties. Certain symbols such as Leviathan one would expect to find repeated. But it is more than that. The blank, expressionless faces of the damned as they are led into torment and their thin, often naked bodies; the bestial face of the Devil, teeth ready to chew his victims, and sometimes depicted chewing Judas Iscariot; the dreary sense of disorder and chaos; these are universal in pictures of hell. Wenhaston's Doom, which was painted by a local monk, is a comparatively modest effort. Many Continental paintings go much further, using anal themes (devils excreting gold pieces into the mouth of usurers, for instance), oral themes (the great greedy mouths of Leviathan and of Satan), and repetitive use of worms threading their way through flesh, bridges which cannot be crossed, menacing woods, demonic hunts, and almost every fantasy which the sado-masochistic mind could imagine. The sense of the hopeless, faceless mob is very strong; there is a stone carving at York Minster of the damned stewing in a cauldron which is strangely reminiscent of a concentration camp photograph, embryonic heads upon wasted bodies. These paintings are the most perfect evocation of the horror of separation, and of oral and anal fixation, with their treadmill of perversion, which is truly damnation for those who must endure it. The monastic artists projected the horror of it into a future state – it must have been too agonising to recognise that Hell, like the Kingdom of Heaven, is within us.

They projected the joy marvellously, too. In Paradise there were many fountains, and gracious femininity presides in the form of a beautiful madonna in her *hortus conclusus*. Adam and Eve recalled an age of lost innocence. It was a Garden of Delights, luminous with order, satisfaction, joy and plenty.

And so they built Heaven and Hell out of very simple images – images which sprang from memories of the man and the woman, the mother and the child, the garden that is the womb on the one hand, and from the experience of fear, insatiable appetite, separation, on the other.

'What did the devil do else, or what was his going astray and his fall else, but that he claimed for himself to be also somewhat, and would have it that somewhat was his, and somewhat was due to him? This setting up of a claim and his I and Me and Mine, these were his going astray, and his fall. And thus it is to this day.

'What else did Adam do but this same thing? . . . I say, it was because of his claiming something for his own, and because of his I, Mine, Me, and the like . . . A man should so stand free, being quit of himself, that is, of his I, and Me, and Self, and Mine and the like, that in all things, he should no more seek or regard himself, than if he did not exist, and should take as little account of himself as if he were not, and another had done all his works . . . Hereby we may mark what disobedience is: to wit, that a man maketh some account of himself, and thinketh that he is, and knoweth and can do somewhat, and seeketh himself and his own ends in the things around him, and hath regard to and loveth himself, and the like . . . Nothing burneth in hell but self-will.'[7]

Music for the Passion. 'I seen them, I seen them, hanging on the old barbed wire.' And the cry under L.S.D. – 'Christ is us, Christ is us.'

XV

'For seven years Gautama had struggled by the traditional means of yoga and *tapas*, contemplation and ascesis, to penetrate the cause of man's enslavement to *maya*, to find release from the vicious circle of clinging-to-life (*trishna*) which is like trying to make the hand grasp itself. All his efforts had been in vain. The eternal *atman*, the real Self, was not to be found. However much he concentrated upon his own mind to find its root and ground, he found only his own effort to concentrate. The evening before his awakening he simply "gave up", relaxed his ascetic diet, and ate some nourishing food.

'Thereupon he felt at once that a profound change was coming over him. He sat beneath the tree, vowing never to rise until he had attained the supreme awakening, and — according to tradition — sat all through the night until the first glimpse of the morning star suddenly provoked a state of perfect clarity and understanding. This was *anuttara samyak sambodhi*, "unexcelled, complete awakening", liberation from *maya* and from the everlasting Round of birth-and-death (*samsara*), which goes on and on for as long as a man tries in any way whatsoever to grasp at his own life.

'Yet the actual content of this experience was never and could never be put into words . . . In its own tradition, Zen

maintains that the Buddha transmitted awakening to his chief
disciple by holding up a flower and remaining silent . . .'[1]

'After Jesus busted outa the grave
He met two of his gang on a road.
Man! were they ever spooked and surprised.
They ran like crazy to the place where the other guys were.
And started to tell who they seen.
Before they could say much, bingo!
Jesus was there,
Came right through the door,
And they couldn't figure that out either,
He said "Peace!" . . .
So Jesus says
"What buggin' you?
I ain't no ghost."
"See, I got hands
And feet just like you guys
Go ahead, touch me and see
You know seein' is believin'."
Well, they couldn't fight that; so they believed,
But, man, were they still surprised.
Just about then Jesus says,
"What cha got to eat? I'm hungry."
So they gave him some fish fry.
One of the Jesus gang was not there—
He musta been real beat
And was out hanging around the corner
Or maybe out tracking another gang.
He thought that the Jesus gang was all washed up anyway.

... The rest of them say,
"Well, look who's here
Mr. Sad Puss hisself—
Where ya been?"
"Betcha can't guess who was here."
Thomas says, "So who cares?"
The rest of them says, "Jesus was here."
Thomas says,
"What a matter with you guys,
You trying to be funny or something?" '[2]

'And it came to pass, as he sat at meat with them, he took bread, and blessed it, and brake, and gave to them.

'And their eyes were opened, and they knew him; and he vanished out of their sight.'[3]

Transformation. Children's stories are full of this, for example, the Ugly Duckling, Beauty and the Beast, the Frog Prince. In the case of the Ugly Duckling and the Frog Prince, the key to the story is miscalculation—an experience common in everyday life. We do not know all the facts of a situation—some of the more optimistic ones have been accidentally withheld from us. Suddenly all is made plain—we are really a swan who had mistaken its true nature, and the slimy frog who appeared to threaten us is really a prince whom we can love. Beauty and the Beast goes much deeper than this. It is a salvation story. Goodness surrenders herself in order to pay a debt of honour. She advances into a situation of horror, ugliness and despair, in which she is overcome by revulsion. When she sees the Beast dying of loneliness, love and pity flow through her and she embraces him forgetting his ugliness. He is at once transformed.

In his own eyes, or in hers? If, as is sometimes said, Beauty and the Beast is an incest-myth, then Beast is the husband who comes between the daughter and her beloved father. When she can leave her father voluntarily — not just to please him — and forget herself in love for Beast, then all is changed. Her projection of him as ugly and dangerous is withdrawn and relationship begins. But goodness and niceness were not enough to get her to the point of resurrection. Darkness, agony, the crucifixion of hope are what bring about her joy.

'Now may every living thing, young or old, weak or strong, living near or far, known or unknown, living or departed or yet unborn, may every living thing be full of bliss.'[4]

> 'love is more thicker than forget
> more thinner than recall
> more seldom than a wave is wet
> more frequent than to fail
>
> it is most mad and moonly
> and less it shall unbe
> than all the sea which only
> is deeper than the sea
>
> love is less always than to win
> less never than alive
> less bigger than the least begin
> less littler than forgive

it is most sane and sunly
and more it cannot die
than all the sky which only
is higher than the sky.'[5]

The moon looked so gentle and peaceful from a distance, that men associated her with femininity. Close to, she appeared harsher, and when men arrived on her the landscape was arid, desolate, sterile. The inward journey follows this pattern in reverse. To begin with there is nothing to be seen but deadness, dust, craters, loneliness. But when we learn to live in the desert, then all is transformed into beauty and life. Mare Tranquillitatis. Mare Serenitatis. Mare Fecunditatis.

'One short step for man . . .' This is what those who make the inward journey undertake.

INDEX OF SOURCES

INDEX OF SOURCES

Chapter I
1. Ch'ing-yuan in *The Way of Zen*, Alan Watts, Penguin.
2. *Beowulf*, David Wright (tr.), Penguin.
3. *Beyond Theology*, Alan Watts, Hodder and Stoughton.
4. *Epic of Gilgamesh*, N. K. Sandars (tr.), Penguin.

Chapter II
1. *A pamphlet on leprosy*, R. V. Wardekar.

Chapter III
1. 'Love is a place' in *No Thanks*, E. E. Cummings, MacGibbon and Kee.
2. *The Archetypal World of Henry Moore*, Erich Neumann, Routledge and Kegan Paul.
3. *Who's Afraid of Virginia Woolf?*, Edward Albee, Penguin.
4. 'Warm are the still and lucky miles' in *Collected Shorter Poems, 1927–57*, W. H. Auden, Faber and Faber.
5. 'I carry your heart' in *Poems*, E. E. Cummings, MacGibbon and Kee.
6. 'Love is a spring at which' in *One Times One*, E. E. Cummings, MacGibbon and Kee.
7. 'I reckon the first day I saw those eyes', Charles Cotton.
8. 'The Riddle' in *Collected Shorter Poems, 1927–57*, W. H. Auden, Faber and Faber.
9. 'Leap before you look' in *Collected Shorter Poems, 1927–57*, W. H. Auden, Faber and Faber.

Chapter IV
1. *Tao te ching*, Lao Tzu (tr. D. C. Lau), Penguin.
2. *Tao te ching*, Lao Tzu (tr. D. C. Lau), Penguin.

3. 'Wand'ring in this world', Michaell Cavendish.
4. *East Coker*, T. S. Eliot, Faber and Faber.
5. *Tao te ching*, Lao Tzu (tr. D. C. Lau), Penguin.
6. Broadcast by Archbishop Anthony Bloom, Metropolitan of Sourozh.
7. *The Way of Zen*, Alan Watts, Penguin.
8. 'One's not half two' in *One Times One*, E. E. Cummings, Mac-Gibbon and Kee.
9. *The Divided Self*, R. D. Laing, Penguin.
10. *The Way of Zen*, Alan Watts, Penguin.
11. *Tao te ching*, Lao Tzu (tr. D. C. Lau), Penguin.
12. Psalm 103: 15–16, *Jerusalem Bible*.
13. *Insearch*, James Hillman, Hodder and Stoughton.

Chapter V
1. *Turning On*, Rasa Gustaitis, Weidenfeld and Nicolson.
2. Exodus 33: 18–22.
3. *A Writer's Diary*, Virginia Woolf, Hogarth Press.
4. *Tao te ching*, Lao Tzu (tr. D. C. Lau), Penguin.
5. 'Love is a spring at which' in *One Times One*, E. E. Cummings, MacGibbon and Kee.

Chapter VI
1. *Tao te ching*, Lao Tzu (tr. D. C. Lau), Penguin.
2. Honorius of Autun.
3. *Revelations of Divine Love*, Julian of Norwich (tr. Clifton Wolters), Penguin.
4. *The Divided Self*, R. D. Laing, Penguin.
5. *The Priest*, Beatrix Beck, Michael Joseph.
6. *Man and His Symbols*, M. L. Franz, Ed. C. G. Jung, Aldus Books.
7. *Insearch*, James Hillman, Hodder and Stoughton.

Chapter VII
1. *Insearch*, James Hillman, Hodder and Stoughton.

Chapter VIII
1. *Tao te ching*, Lao Tzu (tr. D. C. Lau), Penguin.
2. Lang's Homer.

3. *Pensées*, Pascal (tr. J. M. Cohen), Penguin.
4. *Gravity and Grace*, Simone Weil, Routledge and Kegan Paul.
5. *The Priest*, Beatrix Beck, Michael Joseph.
6. The Didache in *Early Christian Writings*, Maxwell Staniforth (tr.), Penguin.
7. *Beyond Theology*, Alan Watts, Hodder and Stoughton.
8. 'Hate blows a bubble of despair' in *Poems*, E. E. Cummings, MacGibbon and Kee.
9. *The Cage*, Dan Billany and David Dowie, Panther.
10. 'When faces called flowers float out of the ground' in *Xaipe*, E. E. Cummings, MacGibbon and Kee.

Chapter X
1. *Beyond Theology*, Alan Watts, Hodder and Stoughton.

Chapter XII
1. *Elected Silence*, Thomas Merton, Burns and Oates.
2. *The Cell*, Thomas Merton, published in *Sobornost'*.

Chapter XIV
1. 'Musée des Beaux Arts' in *Collected Shorter Poems, 1927–57*, W. H. Auden, Faber and Faber.
2. *Arrow in the Blue*, Arthur Koestler, Collins.
3. Isaiah 54: 1–13.
4. Joel 2: 25.
5. 'What if a much of a which of a wind' in *One Times One*, E. E. Cummings, MacGibbon and Kee.
6. *The Possessed*, F. Dostoevsky (tr. Constance Garnett), Everyman.
7. *Theologica Germanica*, S. Winkworth (tr.), Stuart and Watkins.

Chapter XV
1. *The Way of Zen*, Alan Watts, Penguin.
2. *God is for Real, Man*, Carl Burke, Fontana Books.
3. St. Luke 24: 30-31,
4. Buddhist prayer
5. 'Love is more thicker than forget' in *Poems*, E. E. Cummings, MacGibbon and Kee.